Responsive Web Design with HTML5 and CSS3 Essentials

Design and deliver an optimal user experience for all devices

Alex Libby

Gaurav Gupta

Asoj Talesra

[PACKT] open source
PUBLISHING   community experience distilled

BIRMINGHAM - MUMBAI

Responsive Web Design with HTML5 and CSS3 Essentials

First published: August 2016

Production reference: 1240816

Published by Packt Publishing Ltd.
Livery Place
35 Livery Street
Birmingham
B3 2PB, UK.
ISBN 978-1-78355-307-5

www.packtpub.com

Credits

Authors

Alex Libby

Gaurav Gupta

Asoj Talesra

Reviewer

Sasan Seydnejad

Commissioning Editor

Kartikey Pandey

Acquisition Editor

Larissa Pinto

Content Development Editor

Sachin Karnani

Technical Editor

Pranav Kukreti

Copy Editor

Charlotte Carneiro

Project Coordinators

Nikhil Nair

Ritika Manoj

Proofreader

Safis Editing

Indexer

Hemangini Bari

Graphics

Abhinash Sahu

Production Coordinator

Arvindkumar Gupta

About the Authors

Alex Libby has a background in IT support. He has been involved in supporting end users for almost 20 years in a variety of different environments; a recent change in role now sees Alex working as an MVT test developer for a global distributor based in the UK. Although Alex gets to play with different technologies in his day job, his first true love has always been with the open source movement, and in particular experimenting with CSS/CSS3, jQuery, and HTML5. To date, Alex has written 11 books on subjects such as jQuery, HTML5 Video, SASS, and CSS for Packt, and has reviewed several more. *Responsive Web Design with HTML5 and CSS3 Essentials* is Alex's twelfth book for Packt, and second completed as a collaboration project.

> *Writing books has always been rewarding. It's a great way to learn new technologies and give back something to others who have yet to experience them. My thanks must go to Packt and my coauthors for letting me review and assist with editing this book. My special thanks must also go to family and friends for their support too—it helps get through the late nights!*

Gaurav Gupta is a young and budding IT professional and has a good amount of experience of working on web and cross-platform application development and testing. He is a versatile developer and a tester and is always keen to learn new technologies to be updated in this domain. Passion about his work makes him stand apart from other developers.

Even at a relatively early stage of his career, he is a published author of two books, named *Mastering HTML5 Forms* and *Mastering Mobile Test Automation* with Packt Publishing.

A graduate in computer science, he currently works for a reputed Fortune 500 company and has developed and tested several web and mobile applications for the internal use.

Gaurav is a native of Chandigarh, India, and currently lives in Pune, India.

> *First of all, I would like to thank the almighty and my family, who have always guided me to walk on the right path in life. My heartfelt gratitude and indebtedness goes to all those people in my life who gave me constructive criticism, as it contributed directly or indirectly in a significant way toward firing up my zeal to achieve my goals. A special thanks to my sister, Anjali, who is a constant support, always.*

Asoj Talesra is an enthusiastic software developer with strong technical background. As a hybrid mobile app developer, he is responsible for crafting and developing intuitive, responsive web pages, and mobile apps using HTML5, CSS3, JavaScript, AngularJS, jQuery, jQuery Mobile, Xamarin, and Appcelerator Titanium. He works with a Fortune 500 company, and is well experienced in the areas of banking, quality and compliance, and audit.

At the very first, I'd like to thank Gaurav Gupta for advising me with such an amazing opportunity. The astounding encouragement and support from my family and friends is something I'm really indebted to, and I owe each one of you a part of this. I'd also like to thank Apurva and Poonam especially, for their contributions and feedback that helped me a lot shaping up this book.

We wish to extend our sincere gratitude to the team from Packt Publishing and the technical reviewers for their valuable suggestions, which proved extremely helpful in making this a better book for the readers. Our special thanks to our mentors, colleagues, and friends for sharing their experiences, which have proved very valuable in making this book better oriented toward the real-world challenges faced.

- Gaurav Gupta and Asoj Talesra

About the Reviewer

Sasan Seydnejad has more than a decade of experience in web UI and frontend application development using JavaScript, CSS, and HTML in .NET and ASP.NET environments. He specializes in modular SPA design and implementation, responsive mobile-friendly user interfaces, AJAX, client architecture, and UX design, using HTML5, CSS3, and their related technologies. He implements framework-less and framework-based applications using Node.js, MongoDB, Express.js, and AngularJS. He is the holder of the US patent for a user interface for a multidimensional data store—US Patent 6907428.

www.PacktPub.com

eBooks, discount offers, and more

Did you know that Packt offers eBook versions of every book published, with PDF and ePub files available? You can upgrade to the eBook version at www.PacktPub.com and as a print book customer, you are entitled to a discount on the eBook copy. Get in touch with us at customercare@packtpub.com for more details.

At www.PacktPub.com, you can also read a collection of free technical articles, sign up for a range of free newsletters and receive exclusive discounts and offers on Packt books and eBooks.

https://www2.packtpub.com/books/subscription/packtlib

Do you need instant solutions to your IT questions? PacktLib is Packt's online digital book library. Here, you can search, access, and read Packt's entire library of books.

Why subscribe?

- Fully searchable across every book published by Packt
- Copy and paste, print, and bookmark content
- On demand and accessible via a web browser

Table of Contents

Preface

A question—how many devices do you own that can access the Internet?

As a user, I'll bet the answer is likely to be quite a few; this includes smart TVs, cell phones, and the like. As developers, it is up to us to provide a user experience that works on multiple devices. Welcome to the world of responsive design!

Responsive design is not only all about creating a great user experience, but one that works well on multiple different devices, from a simple online ordering process for tickets, right through to an extensive e-commerce system. Many of the tips you see throughout the course of this book don't require extensive changes to your existing development methodology. In many cases, it's enough to make some simple changes to begin building responsive sites.

Creating responsive sites can open up a real world of opportunity for you; over the course of this book, I'll introduce you to the essential elements that you need to be aware of when designing responsively, and provide you with examples and plenty of tips to help get you started with creating responsive designs.

Are you ready to get started? Here's hoping the answer is yes. If so, let's make a start.

What this book covers

Chapter 1, *Introducing Responsive Web Design*, kicks off our journey into the world of responsive design, with an introduction into the basics of the concept; we explore the importance of RWD in today's environment and examine how it works as a concept.

Chapter 2, *Creating Fluid Layouts*, takes a look at creating flexible grid layouts as a key element of our design process; we explore the benefits of using them, and take a look at creating some examples using prebuilt styles.

Chapter 3, *Adding Responsive Media*, walks us through how to make our media responsive. We cover some of the tips and tricks available for use and examine why, in some cases, it is preferable to host content externally (such as videos)—if only to save on bandwidth costs!

Chapter 4, *Exploring Media Queries*, leads us to explore media queries and how we can use them to control what content is displayed at particular screen width settings. We cover the basics of creating breakpoints and examine why these should be based around where content breaks in our design and not simply for specific devices we want to support.

Chapter 5, *Testing and Optimizing for Performance*, rounds off our journey through the essentials of responsive web design with a look at how we can test and optimize our code for efficiency. We explore some of the reasons why pages load slowly, how we can measure our performance, and understand why even though the same tricks can be applied to any site. It's even more critical that we incorporate them when designing responsively.

What you need for this book

All you need to work through most of the examples in this book is a simple text or code editor, an Internet browser, and Internet access. Many of the demos use Google Chrome, so it is ideal if you have this installed; other browsers can be used, although there may be instances where you have to change the steps accordingly.

Who this book is for

The book is for frontend developers who are familiar with HTML5 and CSS3, but want to understand the essential elements of responsive web design. To get the most out of this book, you should have a good knowledge of HTML and CSS3; JavaScript or jQuery are not required for the purposes of running the demos in this book or understanding the code.

Conventions

In this book, you will find a number of text styles that distinguish between different kinds of information. Here are some examples of these styles and an explanation of their meaning.

Code words in text, database table names, folder names, filenames, file extensions, pathnames, dummy URLs, user input, and Twitter handles are shown as follows: "Go ahead and extract a copy of `coffee.html` and save it to our project area."

A block of code is set as follows:

```
img {
    max-width: 100%;
    height: auto;
}
```

When we wish to draw your attention to a particular part of a code block, the relevant lines or items are set in bold:

```
@media only screen and (min-device-width: 768px) and (max-device-width : 1024px) and (orientation : landscape)
```

New terms and **important words** are shown in bold. Words that you see on the screen, for example, in menus or dialog boxes, appear in the text like this: "Click on the cog, then select **Share and embed** map"

Warnings or important notes appear in a box like this.

Tips and tricks appear like this.

Reader feedback

Feedback from our readers is always welcome. Let us know what you think about this book-what you liked or disliked. Reader feedback is important for us as it helps us develop titles that you will really get the most out of. To send us general feedback, simply e-mail feedback@packtpub.com, and mention the book's title in the subject of your message. If there is a topic that you have expertise in and you are interested in either writing or contributing to a book, see our author guide at www.packtpub.com/authors.

Customer support

Now that you are the proud owner of a Packt book, we have a number of things to help you to get the most from your purchase.

Downloading the example code

You can download the example code files for this book from your account at http://www.packtpub.com. If you purchased this book elsewhere, you can visit http://www.packtpub.com/support and register to have the files e-mailed directly to you.

You can download the code files by following these steps:

1. Log in or register to our website using your e-mail address and password.
2. Hover the mouse pointer on the **SUPPORT** tab at the top.
3. Click on **Code Downloads & Errata**.
4. Enter the name of the book in the **Search** box.
5. Select the book for which you're looking to download the code files.
6. Choose from the drop-down menu where you purchased this book from.
7. Click on **Code Download**.

Once the file is downloaded, please make sure that you unzip or extract the folder using the latest version of:

- WinRAR / 7-Zip for Windows
- Zipeg / iZip / UnRarX for Mac
- 7-Zip / PeaZip for Linux

The code bundle for the book is also hosted on GitHub at `https://github.com/PacktPubl ishing/Responsive-Web-Design-with-HTML5-and-CSS3-Essentials`. We also have other code bundles from our rich catalog of books and videos available at `https://github.com/P acktPublishing/`. Check them out!

Downloading the color images of this book

We also provide you with a PDF file that has color images of the screenshots/diagrams used in this book. The color images will help you better understand the changes in the output. You can download this file from `https://www.packtpub.com/sites/default/files/down loads/ResponsiveWebDesignwithHTML5andCSS3Essentials_ColorImages.pdf`.

Errata

Although we have taken every care to ensure the accuracy of our content, mistakes do happen. If you find a mistake in one of our books-maybe a mistake in the text or the code-we would be grateful if you could report this to us. By doing so, you can save other readers from frustration and help us improve subsequent versions of this book. If you find any errata, please report them by visiting `http://www.packtpub.com/submit-errata`, selecting your book, clicking on the **Errata Submission Form** link, and entering the details of your errata. Once your errata are verified, your submission will be accepted and the errata will be uploaded to our website or added to any list of existing errata under the Errata section of that title.

To view the previously submitted errata, go to `https://www.packtpub.com/books/conten` `t/support` and enter the name of the book in the search field. The required information will appear under the **Errata** section.

Piracy

Piracy of copyrighted material on the Internet is an ongoing problem across all media. At Packt, we take the protection of our copyright and licenses very seriously. If you come across any illegal copies of our works in any form on the Internet, please provide us with the location address or website name immediately so that we can pursue a remedy.

Please contact us at `copyright@packtpub.com` with a link to the suspected pirated material.

We appreciate your help in protecting our authors and our ability to bring you valuable content.

Questions

If you have a problem with any aspect of this book, you can contact us at `questions@packtpub.com`, and we will do our best to address the problem.

1
Introducing Responsive Web Design

The concept of web design used to be simple—designers would develop content for a popular desktop screen, using a layout which works for most devices to produce well laid-out and cohesive pages.

With changes in technologies and the introduction of mobile devices, the whole experience changed—gone are the days when a static layout would suffice. In its place came a need for content that responded to the available screen real estate, with elements automatically resized or hidden, according to the device being used. This forms the basis for a technique popularized by Ethan Marcotte, which we now know as **responsive web design (RWD)**. Throughout the course of this chapter, we will begin to explore what this means, and understand some of the principles that are key to this concept.

In this chapter, we will cover the following topics:

- Getting started with RWD
- Understanding the elements of RWD
- Understanding the importance of RWD
- Exploring how RWD works
- Setting up a development workflow
- Exploring best practice and common errors

Curious? Let's get started!

Getting started with RWD

If one had to describe RWD in a sentence, then responsive design describes how the content is displayed across various screens and devices such as mobiles, tablets, phablets, or desktops. To understand what this means, let's use water as an example. The property of water is that it takes the shape of the container in which it is poured. It is an approach in which a website or a webpage adjusts its layout according to the size or resolution of the screen dynamically. This ensures that users get the best experience while using the website.

We develop a single website that uses a single code base. This will contain fluid, flexible images, proportion-based grids, fluid images, or videos and CSS3 media queries to work across multiple devices and device resolutions. The key to making them work is the use of percentage values, in place of fixed units such as pixels or ems-based sizes.

The best part of this is that we can use this technique without the knowledge or need of server based/backend solutions; to see it in action, we can use Packt's website as an example. Go ahead and browse `https://www.packtpub.com/web-development/mastering-html5-forms`; this is what we will see as a desktop view:

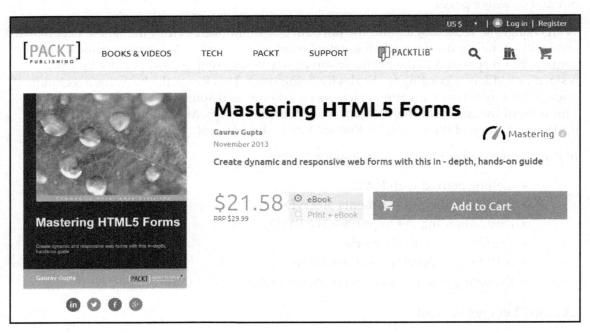

The mobile view for the same website shows this, if viewed on a smaller device:

We can clearly see the same core content is being displayed (that is, an image of the book, the buy button, pricing details, and information about the book), but elements such as the menu have been transformed into a single drop-down located in the top-left corner. This is what RWD is all about—producing a flexible design that adapts according to which device we choose to use, in a format that suits the device being used.

Let's try it with another technology site; I am sure some of you are familiar with the A List Apart site (hosted at `http://alistapart.com` and founded by the well-known Jeffery Zeldman):

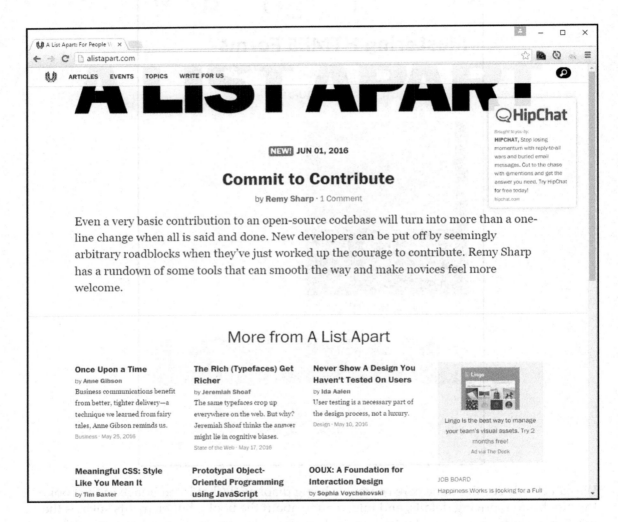

Try resizing your browser window. This is a perfect example of how a simple text site can reflow content with minimal changes; in place of the text menu, we now have the hamburger icon (which we will cover later in this chapter):

While the text in this site realigns with minimal difficulty, it seems that the top image doesn't work so well—it hasn't resized as part of the change, so will appear cut off on smaller devices.

Although this may seem a complex task to achieve, in reality it boils down to following some simple principles; how these are implemented will ultimately determine the success of our site. We've seen some in use as part of viewing Packt's and A List Apart's sites at various sizes—let's take a moment to explore the principles of how responsive design works, and why it is an important part of creating a site for the modern Internet.

Exploring how RWD works

For some, the creation of what we now know as RWD is often associated with Ethan Marcotte, although its true origins date from earlier when the site Audi.com was first created, which had an adaptive viewport area as a result of limitations within IE at the time.

If one had to describe what RWD is, then Ethan sums it up perfectly:

Rather than tailoring disconnected designs to each of an ever-increasing number of web devices, we can treat them as facets of the same experience. We can design for an optimal viewing experience, but embed standards-based technologies into our designs to make them not only more flexible, but more adaptive to the media that renders them. In short, we need to practice responsive web design.

In a nutshell, RWD is about presenting an experience for customers on different devices that allows them to interact with your business. It is important to note though that the experience does not have to use the same process; it is more important that the customer can achieve the same result, even though they may arrive using a different route. So, how does RWD work?

RWD is a set of principles we should follow, but the overriding philosophy is about making content fluid. Gone are fixed values, at least for elements on the page; in their place, we use percentage values or em/rem units. Our page layout will use a fluid grid, which resizes automatically depending on the available viewport space.

One key concept that will help determine the success of our site is not one we might automatically associate with responsive design, but nevertheless will help: divine proportion.

Divine proportion, or the Golden Ratio as it is often known, is a way of defining proportions that are aesthetically pleasing—it is perfect for setting the right proportions for a responsive layout. The trick behind it is to use this formula:

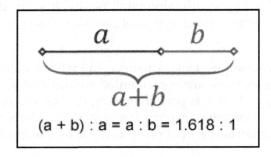

$$(a + b) : a = a : b = 1.618 : 1$$

Imagine we have a layout that is 960px wide, which we want to split into two parts, called **a** and **b**. Divine proportion states that the size of **a** must be **1.618** times the size of **b**.

To arrive at our column widths, we must complete the following calculations:

1. Divide the width of our site (960px) by 1.618. This gives 593px (rounded to the nearest integer).
2. Subtract 593px from 960px. This gives 367px.

It's a simple formula, but one that will help improve the communication of content for your site—we're not forced to have to use it though; sites are available on the Internet that don't follow this principle. It does mean that they must ensure that the content is still equally balanced, to give that pleasing effect—this isn't so easy!

The important point here though is that we shouldn't be using fixed pixel values for a responsive site; instead, we can use rem units (which resize better) or ideally percentage values.

To translate this into something more meaningful, we can simply work out the resulting column widths as percentages of the original size. In this instance, 593px equates to 62% and 367px is 38%. That would give us something like this:

```
#wrapper { width: 60rem; }
#sidebar { width: 32%; }
#main { width: 68%; }
```

Okay, a little theoretical, but hopefully you get the idea! It's a simple formula, but a great way to ensure that we arrive at a layout which is properly balanced; using percentage values (or at the very least rem units), will help make our site responsive at the same time.

Understanding the elements of RWD

Now that we've been introduced to RWD, it's important to understand some of the elements that make up the philosophy of what we know as flexible design. A key part of this is understanding the viewport or visible screen estate available to us; in addition to viewports, we must also consider flexible media, responsive text and grids, and media queries. We will cover each in more detail later in the book, but to start with, let's take a quick overview of the elements that make up RWD.

Controlling the viewport

A key part of RWD is working with the viewport or visible content area on a device. If we're working with desktops, then it is usually the resolution; this is not the case for mobile devices.

There is a temptation to reach for JavaScript (or a library such as jQuery) to set values such as viewport width or height, but there is no need, as we can do this using CSS:

```
<meta name="viewport" content="width=device-width">
```

or using this directive:

```
<meta name="viewport" content="width=device-width, initial-scale=1">
```

This means that the browser should render the width of the page to the same width as the browser window—if for example the latter is 480px, then the width of the page will be 480px. To see what a difference that not setting a viewport can have, take a look at this example screenshot:

Most Persons Never Noticed the Increase

"Granser," he announced, "you make me sick with your gabble. Why don't you tell about the Red Death? If you ain't going to, say so, an' we'll start back for camp."

The old man looked at him and silently began to cry. The weak tears of age rolled down his cheeks and all the feebleness of his eighty-seven years showed in his grief-stricken countenance.

This example was created from displaying some text in Chrome, in iPhone 6 Plus emulation mode, but without a viewport. Now, let's view the same text, but this time with a viewport directive set:

Most Persons Never Noticed the Increase

"Granser," he announced, "you make me sick with your gabble. Why don't you tell about the Red Death? If you ain't going to, say so, an' we'll start back for camp."

The old man looked at him and silently began to cry. The weak tears of age rolled down his cheeks and all the feebleness of his eighty-seven years showed in his grief-stricken countenance.

Even though this is a simple example, do you notice any difference? Yes, the title color has changed, but more importantly the width of our display has increased. This is all part of setting a viewport—browsers frequently assume we want to view content as if we're on a desktop PC. If we don't tell it that the viewport area has been shrunk in size (and that we have not set the scaling correctly), it will try to shoehorn all of the content into a smaller size. This will result in a page that will appear to be zoomed out, which doesn't work very well!

It's critical, therefore, that we set the right viewport for our design, and that we allow it to scale up or down in size, irrespective of the device. We will explore this in more detail, in `Chapter 2`, *Creating Fluid Layouts*.

Creating flexible grids

When designing responsive sites, we can either create our own layout or use a grid system already created for use, such as Bootstrap. The key here though is ensuring that the mechanics of our layout sizes and spacing are set according to the content we want to display for our users, and that when the browser is resized in width, it realigns itself correctly.

For many developers, the standard unit of measure has been pixel values; a key part of responsive design is to make the switch to using percentage and em (or preferably rem) units. The latter scales better than standard pixels, although there is a certain leap of faith needed to get accustomed to working with the replacements!

Making media responsive

Two key parts of our layout are of course images and text—the former though can give designers a bit of a headache, as it is not enough to simply use large images and set overflow—hidden to hide the parts that are not visible!

Images in a responsive site must be as flexible as the grid used to host them—for some, this may be a big issue if the site is very content heavy; now is a good time to consider if some of that content is no longer needed, and can be removed from the site. We can of course simply apply `display: none` to any image which shouldn't be displayed, according to the viewport set. However, this isn't a good idea though, as content still has to be downloaded before styles can be applied; it means we're downloading more than is necessary! Instead, we should assess the level of content, make sure it is fully optimized and then apply percentage values so it can be resized automatically to a suitable size when the browser viewport changes.

Constructing suitable breakpoints

With content and media in place, we must turn our attention to media queries—there is a temptation to create queries that suit specific devices, but this can become a maintenance headache.

We can avoid the headache by designing queries based on where the content breaks rather than for specific devices—the trick to this is to start small and gradually enhance the experience, with the use of media queries:

```
<link rel="stylesheet" media="(max-device-width: 320px)" href="mobile.css"
/>
<link rel="stylesheet" media="(min-width: 1600px)" href="widescreen.css" />
```

We should aim for around 75 characters per line, to maintain an optimal length for our content.

Appreciating the importance of RWD

So – we've explored how RWD works, and some of the key elements that make up this philosophy; question is, why is it so important to consider using it? There are several benefits to incorporating a responsive capability to our sites, which include the following:

- It is easier for users to interact with your site, if it is designed to work with multiple devices.
- Creating a single site that caters to multiple devices may in itself require more effort, but the flip side of this is that we're only developing one site, not multiple versions.
- Constructing a site that works based on how much can be displayed in a specific viewport is a more effective way to render content on screen than relying on browser agent strings, which can be falsified and error prone.
- RWD is able to cater to future changes. If we plan our site carefully, we can construct media queries that cater for devices already in use and ones yet to be released for sale.

Making our site accessible and intuitive

Accessibility plays a key role in responsive design. Our content should be as intuitive as possible, with every single piece of information easy to access. Responsive design places great emphasis on making our design self-explanatory; there shouldn't be any doubt as to how to access information on the site.

 In this context, accessibility refers to making our site available on a wide variety of devices; this should not be confused with the need to cater for individuals with disabilities. Making sites accessible for them is equally important, but is not a primary role in RWD.

Even though our mobile version may not contain the same information (which is perfectly accessible), it nonetheless must be engaging, with appealing colors, legible text (at all sizes), and a design that retains visual harmony and balance with our chosen color scheme.

Organizing our content

The success of our site is determined by a host of factors, of which one of these will be how our content is organized in the layout. The content should be organized in such a way that its layout makes it easy to process, is simple and free of clutter, and that we're making full use of the available viewport space for the device we're targeting.

We must also ensure our content is concise—we should aim to get our point across in as few words as possible so that mobile users are not wasting time with downloading redundant content. Keeping our options simple is essential – if we make it too complicated, with lots of links or categories, then this will increase the time it takes for visitors to make decisions, and ultimately only serve to confuse them!

At this point, it is worth pointing out something – over time, you may come across the phrase **adaptive design**, when talking about responsive design. There is a subtle but key difference between the two, and either can be used as a principle when constructing our site. Let's take a moment to explore what each means, and the differences that might affect how we go about constructing our sites.

Comparing RWD to adaptive design

So, what is adaptive design, and how does it differ to responsive design?

Responsive design is about making one design fit many devices—it requires us to create the optimal viewing solution for a site, no matter which device we care to use. This means that we should not have to resize, scroll, or pan more than is absolutely necessary; if for example our page width doesn't fit the screen we're using, then our design isn't right! Ultimately though, we can view responsive design as a ball that grows or shrinks in size automatically, to fit several sizes of hoops.

Staying with the hoop analogy, adaptive design works on the principle that we have multiple layouts that are available for use; the browser will select the right one to use, based on detecting which type of device is in use. In this instance, we would be putting several different balls through different sized hoops, depending on the size of hoop in use. The key difference though is that responsive design focuses on client-side development; adaptive design in the main uses server-side detection to display the best-fitting page, based on the device being used to browse the site.

For the purpose of this book, we will work on using responsive design throughout all of the examples used within the text.

Now that we understand the importance of using RWD and how it differs from adaptive design, let's really begin on our journey; our first step is to get our development environment prepared for use. At this point, you might be expecting to download lots of different plugins or be using libraries such as jQuery. You might be in for a little surprise!

Preparing our development environment

Okay, we've covered enough general background; time to get more practical!

There are many tools available to help us, when constructing responsive sites; this of course includes tools such as JavaScript or jQuery, but also plugins such as FitVids (to manage videos, responsively) or ResponsiveSlides for creating responsive carousels.

However, we're not going to use any of them. All we need is a text editor and a browser, and nothing more! We're not going to download anything as part of completing the exercises in this book.

Yes, I hear those exclamations of incredulity. I must have lost my marbles, I hear you say. There is a very good reason for this approach though; let me explain:

On too many occasions, I see instances where we simply reach for the latest plugin to help us achieve a result. Ordinarily, there is nothing wrong with this; after all, time pressures frequently mean that we can't afford the time to take a more considered approach.

However, I believe we've become lazy. There is no need for many of the tools that are available, when building responsive sites. It's time to go back to basics; throughout the course of this book, we're going to prove that we can build the basics of responsive functionality, with nothing more than a simple text editor and a browser for viewing.

There are some caveats to this approach though, that we should bear in mind:

- Much of what we construct won't work in some older browsers—IE9 or below is a good case in point. The question you must ask yourself is: how many people use this for your site? If the percentage is very low, then you can consider dropping them; if not, then you will need to seek a different approach.
- Concentrating on using just HTML and CSS does not mean that we're rejecting other tools outright; if we need to use them, then we need to use them. The question we must ask ourselves though is this: do we really need to use them? Or are we just too lazy to go *old school* and create things from the ground up?

With that aside, there are a couple of administration tasks we need to complete first; we need a project area to store our content. I would recommend creating a folder somewhere on your PC or Mac to store files; I will for the purposes of this book assume you've called it B03568, and that it is stored on the C: drive. If you've stored it somewhere else, then adjust accordingly.

Next up, we will need a copy of the code download that accompanies this book—there will be instances where we won't cover some of the more mundane content, but focus on the really important content; we can get those less critical files from the code download.

Finally, do you have a text editor that you like using? If not, then you might like to look at Sublime Text 3; it is our preferred editor of choice. The real benefit of using it means we can add plugins, such as the REM-PX (available from https://packagecontrol.io/packages/REM%2PX), which is perfect for converting from pixel to rem-based values! (We will cover this more in later chapters).

Okay, onwards we go; the next stage in our journey is to consider a suitable strategy for creating our responsive sites. There is nothing outrageously complex about this, it is more about making some sensible choices as to what approach we should use which bests fit our solution. Let's take a moment to explore what this means in practice.

Considering a suitable strategy

As a developer, I am sure you will be wanting to get stuck into creating your next masterpiece, right? Sounds familiar; after all, that is what helps to pay the bills…

Before we can get into writing code, we must develop some form of strategy, this can be as simple or as complex as befits our requirements. Although there is something to be said for defining ground rules, I've never been one for rigid principles; instead, developing a set of guidelines and principles to follow means that we can be flexible about our approach, while still retaining a sense of consistency.

There are a few guidelines that we should try to incorporate into our development process, these are more about helping to reduce any lack of clarity when developing responsive sites for the first time:

- **Choosing mobile over desktop**: This is not a new idea; it has been around since before responsive design took off as a serious approach to creating sites. The mobile-first concept means that we should develop our content for smaller mobile devices first, before working up to tablets and desktops. At this stage, it is important to be aware of what visitors may be using for your current site; this will help determine which devices we should concentrate on as part of our design.

- **Breakpoints**: Getting these right will be essential to the success of any site we build; not only must we choose the right thresholds for the devices we want to support, but also ensure that the cut-off points do not overlap each other. A common misconception is to develop for standard breakpoints such as desktops or tablets; instead, we should set our breakpoints to kick in when our content breaks within our layout. This screenshot shows the type of thresholds we have to consider in our designs:

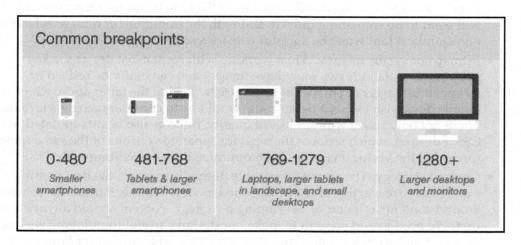

Common breakpoints

0-480	481-768	769-1279	1280+
Smaller smartphones	*Tablets & larger smartphones*	*Laptops, larger tablets in landscape, and small desktops*	*Larger desktops and monitors*

- **The flow of content**: When we start designing for smaller screens, content will naturally be squeezed and begin to flow downwards. This may be tricky to grasp as a concept, if you're used to pixels and points when designing, but it will make sense once you get used to how content will flow downwards in responsive design.

- **Relative units**: This is an important concept in responsive design. It's a case of learning how to make the switch from static values to relative units. Calculating values in percentages means that content will always fit, no matter what the viewport size; for example, the size of a <div> set to 50% means that it will only ever fill 50% of its parent container, no matter what the size of the viewport. It may be a case of building the initial design with static values, but we should try to get into the mindset of converting to use percentages as part of our design process.

- **Max and min values**: A part of using relative values means that our browser won't understand what the lower and upper size limits of each element will be. To work around this, we must set min-width or max-width values; these will ensure that no matter what width our elements are at, they won't go past the limits set in code.

- **Web fonts or system fonts**: If you maintain a desktop version of your site already, and it uses one or more web fonts, then you have an important decision to make: should the mobile site use the same fonts? The reason for asking is because this requires additional content to be downloaded; it will consume extra bandwidth, which will be a concern for devices where this is limited. Bear in mind that anyone using a mobile device is likely to be under time pressure, they will want to do something quickly and with the minimum of fuss, so selecting a non-standard font won't be a useful way forward.

- **Bitmaps or vector images**: When working with responsive designs, a key principle is scalability; we must have images that can easily be resized or swapped for larger or smaller as appropriate. Taking the latter approach on a mobile device isn't wise; a better route would be to consider using vector images. These not only resize without loss of quality, but can also be manipulated using CSS if desired, which reduces the need for separate versions of the same image (provided the vector image has been optimized prior to editing with CSS).

- **Content strategy**: The aim of responsive design is to create the best possible experience, irrespective of the device used to view the site. Part of this centers around content; as a part of developing a strategy, content should always come first. We need to add enough to make our design a useful foundation; we can then add or develop this at a later date, when we add support for larger screens and resolutions.

- **Sketch and prototype**: Once we have worked out our content and a strategy for managing it, it's time to develop the layout. A key part of this should incorporate sketching or wireframing; it will help turn the rough beginnings of a plan into something more solid. Many designers will use PhotoShop, but this is at the risk of wasting lots of billable hours that must be accounted for with the client. Sketching on paper is portable, and has a low visual and content fidelity, which means we can focus on how content interacts, rather than how it looks.

- **Frameworks**: Using a framework in our development can bring several benefits to our development process; it's tried and tested code means that we can cut down on development time, and make use of the grid approach to build and refine our layout around our content. Frameworks will have already been tested across multiple devices, so the debugging time is reduced; we should concentrate on choosing the right framework, based on criteria such as the learning curve required, support, and documentation availability.

> A caveat with using frameworks though is their size; if we go down this route, we should choose carefully which one to use, as many are code heavy and adding extra unnecessary code will make our sites slower.

- **Scalable media**: Images and videos are essential for any site; not only do they help add color, they can also convey more in a smaller space. All of our images must be scalable; it doesn't matter if we swap images out as our resolution increases, or we use a scalable format such as SVG. We need to give consideration to sourcing both standard and hi-resolution versions of our images, to cater for those devices that support the latter; these can either be individual or in the form of image sprites. Our media strategy should also consider using icon fonts, which are perfect for small, repeatable elements such as social media logos.

- **Minification**: If we're building sites to work on devices where bandwidth constraints and limited resources may be a factor, then we must consider minifying our CSS and JavaScript content. Minifying should be a standard part of any development workflow. We can reduce the number of HTTP requests to the server and improve response times. When designing responsively, minification becomes more critical, as we are adding more CSS styles (such as media queries) to cater for different viewports. This will inflate the size of our style sheets even further so anything we can do to help reduce the size, will help encourage takeup of our newly developed responsive site on mobile devices.

As developers, we should have some form of strategy in place when creating our sites; it should not be so rigid as to prevent us changing direction if our existing plans are not working. Whichever way we decide to go, we should always consider an element of best practice in our development workflow; there are a few tips we could use right about now, so let's take a look in more detail.

Exploring best practices

Best practices...ugh...what a phrase!

This is a phrase that is used and abused to death; the irony is that when it is used, it isn't always used correctly either! This said, there are some pointers we can use to help with designing our responsive sites; let's take a look at a few:

- **Use a minimalistic approach**: This is very popular at the moment and perfect for responsive design. It reduces the number of elements we have to realign when screen dimensions change; it also makes editing content and elements easier, if our page content is at a minimum.
- **Always go for a mobile-first strategy**: It is essential to consider what the user experience will be like on a mobile device. The proportion of those who own a mobile device or phone is higher than those who own their own PC; we must make sure that content is both viewable and legible on a smaller screen. Once we've nailed this, we can then extend our design for larger screens.
- **Understand the need for speed**: A slow site is a real turn off for customers; a good guideline to aim for when measuring load times is for around 4–5 seconds. There can be many reasons why a site is slow to load, from slow site feeds to poorly optimized hardware, but one of the easier to rectify is large images. Make sure that you've been through all of the media that is loaded, and checked to ensure it has been fully optimized for your site.
- **Try to keep the site design as clean as possible**: Eliminate anything that is not needed to convey your message. It goes without saying, but why use 20 words, when we can get our message across in 10?
- **Make use of the hamburger icon:** No, I'm not referring to food, irrespective of what size it is (sorry, bad joke!). Instead, make use of it as a consistent point of access to your site. Be mindful though that users may not want to have to keep tapping on it to access everything, so if you have menu items that are frequently used more often, then consider exposing these in your site, and hide anything less important under the hamburger icon.

- **Don't use small button sizes for anything**: Bear in mind that many users will use fingers to tap on icons, so any clickable icons should be large enough to allow accurate tapping and reduce any frustration with accidentally tapping the wrong link.
- **Familiarize yourself with media queries**: As we'll see later in Chapter 4, *Exploring Media Queries*, we can use media queries to control how content is displayed under certain conditions on different devices. These play a key role in responsive design; it's up to us to get the right mix of queries based on what we need to support!

There are plenty more best practices we can follow, but we shouldn't simply follow them blindly; apart from the risk of our sites losing any *stand-out* appeal (that is, all being the same), not all best practice necessarily applies or is even accurate.

Instead, it is worth researching what others have done online; over time, you will begin to see common threads—these are the threads that should form the basis for any discussions you may have with regards to the design of your site.

There are some practices we should follow, not necessarily because they are best practices, but borne more out of common sense; a great example is touch. When we are designing for touch, there are some pointers which we should use that will influence our design, so let's take a look at these in more detail.

Designing for touch

Although there are lots of tips and pointers we can use to help improve our responsive development, there is one subject that is worth exploring in more detail—touch.

Why? The answer is simple—working responsively is not just about writing code; anyone can write code. The difference though, and that which separates great developers from the crowd, is the thought given to how that site looks and works. Care paid at this point will separate exceptional sites from the also-rans; to get a feel for the kind of decisions and thoughts one might go through, let's take a look at what we might have to consider when designing for touch:

- Aim to use the corners. On small screens, the lower left corner is frequently the easiest to access; for tablets, the top corners work better. We must consider putting any call to action buttons in these locations, and adapt our designs to realign automatically if different devices are used.
- Don't make the buttons too small. A good guideline for tap targets (including buttons) is usually around 44 points (or 3.68rem).

- Avoid placing items too closely together to prevent someone accessing the wrong item by mistake. A good starting point for spacing to avoid interface errors is a minimum of 23pt (or 1.92rem).
- Use natural interactions and create navigation that works well with common hand gestures, such as swiping. This screenshot shows some of the example hand gestures we can use, and that we must allow for when constructing our sites:

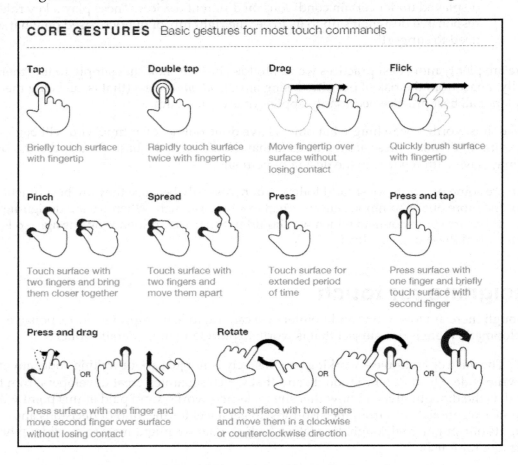

Source: The Next Web (http://www.thenextweb.com)

Hover stages are a no-no in responsive design—these do not exist. Any calls to action should be based around tapping, so make sure your design takes this factor into consideration.

Phew, there are a few things to think of there! The key thing though is that while writing code is easy, creating an effective responsive design takes time and resources, and should always be a continuous affair, so our designs can stay fresh and up to date.

It's time for us to move on to a different subject, now that we've explored some of the guidelines and tips we can use to help with responsive development, it's time for us to consider our workflow. We may already have an established one for producing standard sites, making a shift to incorporate responsive design may require us making some changes to our processes, so let's go and explore what a typical workflow could look like when working with responsive design.

Setting up a development workflow

Before we start on our workflow, let me ask you a question:

Does your workflow process consist of steps such as planning, creating static wireframes, building static designs, adding code then testing, and finally launching your site? Sounds familiar?

If so, then be prepared for a change; using the waterfall process (to which these steps align), doesn't work so well when creating responsive sites; working responsively is all about being agile, as illustrated by the developer Viljami Salminen from 2012:

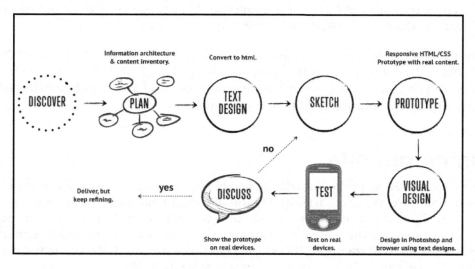

Source: Viljami Salminen, 2012

Although his design dates from 2012, it is still perfectly valid today; before you all put your hands up in horror, let me explain why a waterfall process doesn't work for responsive design:

- We cannot hope to get support for lots of different devices built into our site in one go. We must focus on a small viewport first, before gradually enlarging it to include support for larger devices and finally desktops.
- When working responsively, our focus must be on content first, and not the layout; the reason for this is that our media queries should be built around where content breaks if we change the width of our available viewport. This removes the dependency on building for specific devices, and means that we can build queries that can serve multiple devices.

Our development process needs to be iterative, and focus chiefly on text and media before constructing the layout. Throughout the process, we should keep in constant contact with our client, as part of each iteration; gone are the days of working towards the big reveal! With all of this in mind, let's go through Viljami's illustration in more detail.

Discovering the requirements

This initial stage is the same for any sites, but is particularly important for responsive design, given the different viewport sizes we have to support in our site. It's all about getting to know the client and their requirements. We must get an understanding of our client's business, their competitors, and what they are trying to achieve.

It's at this point we should be asking questions such as, "Why would people come to your site?", "What is the main goal you are trying to achieve?", and "Who are your main competitors?" The more we ask, the more we can understand and therefore better advise our clients on the best solution to fit their requirements.

Planning our site

When we've gathered all of the knowledge needed to construct our site, we now need to plan how it will look. We can start with the initial concept, but rather than work on the layout as we might have done before, we should concentrate on the content elements, and creating user stories and the information architecture. We can then put this together in a rudimentary HTML wireframe. At this stage, layout is less critical; it's key that we get the right view of information, before focusing on where it sits on the page.

Designing the text

At this point, we now need to focus on writing our content in textual form. This often under-rated step is probably the most important of the whole process; without it, people won't come to see the site, and there is no point in designing a layout if we don't know what will fill it! A useful tip is to keep styling to a minimum and to concentrate on the content; at least initially, we can see how it will display in a long, continuous format, and if it works for those who use screen readers. Don't worry though, we can always refine the text during the prototyping stage; at this point, we need something to start with, but it will be unlikely we get it right first time.

Sketching our design

For our next step, forget using PhotoShop; it takes forever and is a real pain to make corrections quickly! The agile process is about making quick and easy changes and there is no better medium than traditional pen and paper. We can even print off the plain text content and sketch around, it if that helps, it will save us hours of development time, and can even help reduce those occasions when you hit the developer's block of…what now?

Prototyping and creating our design

With the design sketched, it's time to create a prototype. This is when we can see how the layout will respond to different viewport sizes and allow us to highlight any potential challenges, or react to any issues that are reported by our client. It's good to be aware of the various breakpoints, but ultimately we should let our content determine where these breakpoints should be set in our design.

We might be used to prototyping our design using PhotoShop, but a better alternative is to switch to using a browser. We can use a service such as Proto.io(`https://proto.io/`) or Froont (`http://froont.com/`). This gives us extra time to get the harder elements right, such as typography; it also helps to remove any constraints that we might have with tools such as PhotoShop.

Testing our design

Although we may still be at a prototype stage, it's important to introduce testing early on. The number of breakpoints we may end up having in our design means that testing on multiple devices will take time! As an alternative to running a big test and reveal, we can instead perform multiple tests and reveals. This has the benefit of reducing the impact of any rollbacks (if something doesn't fit requirements), but also helps to keep the client involved with the project, as they can see progress take place during development.

The one thing we absolutely must do is to test over multiple devices. It's an expensive proposition to maintain a test suite with these devices, so it's worth asking colleagues, friends, and family to see if they can help test for you. They can at least browse the site and help pinpoint where things *don't look right* (to use customer parlance). It's up to us to work out where the root cause is, and implement a fix to help improve the user experience.

Exploring mistakes

With the best will in the world, we are only human; there will be times when we make a mistake! As the playwright Oscar Wilde once said, "*...to err once is human, to err twice is careless.*" Well, in the hope that we don't go that far, there are some common errors that are regularly made when working responsively; let's take a look at the top five candidates:

- **Failing to allow for touch input**: It might seem odd, but failing to allow for touch is surprisingly common! Some users expect a site to *simply work,* and to have a consistent approach across the board both for desktops and mobiles. This will include any mechanism for activating links (such as buttons). What might work on a desktop client will very likely fail on a mobile device. It is absolutely key that we include something to allow mobile users to navigate around a site using touch. This can be achieved (in the main) with CSS3 styling, so there is no excuse!

- **Insisting on a consistent navigation**: A part of creating a successful site will be to have some form of navigation that retains a consistent look and feel across all pages; it does not mean to say that we have to carry this over to mobile devices though! Navigation on a mobile device will of course act differently; we have the added extra of touch input to cater for, as part of our design. At an absolute minimum, links and buttons, along with our choice of typeface and colors should remain consistent; the size of buttons, our visual layout, and how we click on buttons can change.

- **Building in links to non-mobile friendly content**: How many times have you accessed content via a mobile device, only to find it is a huge image or substantial document that has to be downloaded? I'll bet that this irked you. Make sure your content is suitable for downloading on different devices. On a broadband connection for a desktop, we might think nothing of using 100Kb images; try loading these over a 3G connection, and it is easy to see why we need to reconsider what we've previously used on standard broadband connections.

- **Ignoring performance**: In an age of modern broadband connections, it is easy to be complacent about what is made available for download. If we think desktop first, then we will be building ourselves a real problem when it comes to designing our mobile site! We can't compress a desktop environment into a mobile experience—it won't be efficient, will offer poor user experience, and ultimately lead to a drop in conversions in sales. To avoid issues with performance, we should aim to use a minimalistic or *mobile-first* approach, as the basis for our site designs.

- **Testing**: A common error to make is not sufficiently testing our solutions on multiple devices, running them prior to release will uncover any UX issues that need to be resolved before making our solution available for general use. A sticking point is likely to be the question of how many devices we test for. If we have access to analytics for an existing desktop version of the site, then this should give us a starting point we can use to double check our design is working as expected. Failing this, we can make use of device emulators in browsers to run some basic checks. We can also use online testing services, such as MobileTest.me (`http://mobiletest.me`), to ensure our design is working sufficiently to release for wider use.

These common issues can easily be solved with some simple changes to our development workflow process, building at least some of these steps to avoid the grief we may get from these errors, early on, will save a lot of heartache later during development!

Summary

The philosophy that is RWD opens up lots of opportunities for us as designers. With the advent of mobile and other internet-capable devices, it is important to not only make the switch, but also understand how to get it right. We've covered a number of useful topics around RWD, so let's take a moment to reflect on what you've learned in this chapter.

We kicked off with a gentle introduction to RWD, before exploring the basic principles behind making our sites responsive and understanding some of the key elements that make up RWD.

We then moved on to explore the importance of RWD as a set of guiding principles we can follow; we explored how this compares to adaptive design, and that while responsive design can be harder to implement, it is worth the effort over time.

Next up came a look at strategy—we covered the importance of getting this right, along with the different elements that should be considered when making the move toward working responsively. We took a look at some of the best practices that we can follow and called out designing for touch as a key part of these guidelines, to illustrate some of the decisions we need to make during development.

We then rounded out the chapter with an extensive look at creating a development workflow. We explored how we may have to make changes to our existing processes, and some of the topics that have to be incorporated into our development, before discussing some of the points where we might trip us up, if we don't take care over our designs!

Phew, there's a lot of detail there! The great thing though is that we've covered a lot of the strategic considerations we need to make; it's time to put some of this into practice and start building content and layouts. Let's move on and start looking at how we can build flexible grid layouts. This will be the subject of the next chapter in our journey.

2
Creating Fluid Layouts

A key part of our journey through the essentials of responsive design is laying out content on the page—in the early days of the Internet, this was a simple process!

With the advent of mobile devices (and those non-PC devices) that can access the Internet, content layout has become ever more critical; for example, how many images do we have, or do we include content X, or show a summary instead? These are just some of the questions we might ask ourselves. It goes to show that it can open a real can of worms!

To simplify the process, we can use grid or fluid-based layouts. Throughout the course of this chapter, we'll take a look at using them in more detail; we'll start with setting the available viewport, and take it right through to future grid-based layouts.

In this chapter, we will cover the following topics:

- Introducing grid layouts and understanding different types
- Setting the available viewport for use
- Exploring the benefits and mechanics of using grid layouts
- Implementing a prebuilt grid layout
- Exploring the future of grid-based template layouts

Curious? Let's get started!

 Note that the exercises have been designed for the Windows platform, as this is the authors' platform of choice; alter as appropriate if you use a different platform.

Introducing flexible grid layouts

For many years, designers have built layouts of different types; they may be as simple as a calling card site, right through to a theme for a content management system, such as WordPress or Joomla. The meteoric rise of accessing the Internet through different devices means that we can no longer create layouts that are tied to specific devices or sizes—we must be flexible!

To achieve this flexibility requires us to embrace a number of changes in our design process—the first being the type of layout we should create. A key part of this is the use of percentage values to define our layouts; rather than create something from the ground up, we can make use of a predefined grid system that has been tried and tested, as a basis for future designs.

The irony is that there are lots of grid systems vying for our attention, so without further ado, let's make a start by exploring the different types of layouts, and how they compare to responsive designs.

Understanding the different layout types

A problem that has faced web designers for some years is the type of layout their site should use—should it be fluid, fixed width, have the benefits of being elastic, or a hybrid version that draws on the benefits of a mix of these layouts?

The type of layout we choose to use will of course depend on client requirements—making it a fluid layout means we are effectively one step closer to making it responsive; the difference being that the latter uses media queries to allow resizing of content for different devices, not just normal desktops!

To understand the differences, and how responsive layouts compare, let's take a quick look at each in turn:

- **Fixed width layouts**: These are constrained to a fixed width; a good size is around 960px, as this can be split equally into columns, with no remainder. The downside is fixed width makes assumptions about the available viewport area, and if the screen is too small or large, it results in lots of scrolling which affects the user experience.
- **Fluid layouts**: Instead of using static values, we use percentage-based units; it means that no matter what the size of the browser window, our site will adjust accordingly. This removes the problems that surround fixed layouts at a stroke.

- **Elastic layouts**: They are similar to fluid layouts, but the constraints are measured by type or font size, using em or rem units; these are based on the defined font size, so 16px is 1 rem, 32px is 2 rem, and so on. These layouts allow for decent readability, with lines of 45-70 characters; font sizes are resized automatically. We may still see scrollbars appear in some instances, or experience some odd effects if we zoom our page content.
- **Hybrid layouts**: They combine a mix of two or more of these different layout types; this allows us to choose static widths for some elements while others remain elastic or fluid.

In comparison, responsive layouts take fluid layouts a step further, using media queries to not only make our designs resize automatically, but also present different views of our content on multiple devices.

How do we set the available space though, and be sure that our content will zoom in or out as appropriate? Easy—we can do this by adding the viewport directive to our markup; let's go and explore what is required to allow our viewport to resize as needed.

Setting the available viewport for use

When viewing a website on different devices, we of course expect it to resize to the available device width automatically with no loss of *experience*; unfortunately, not every site does this quite the right way or successfully!

To understand why this is important, let's assume we operate a desktop version of our site (one in the 1280+ group in this screenshot), and a mobile equivalent from the 418-768 group:

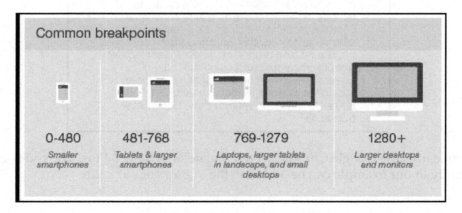

The first stage in making our site responsive is to add the viewport directive; without it, we are likely to end up with a similar effect to this when resizing our sites:

> meta name="viewpo
> width, initial-scale=1
>
> Lorem ipsum dolor sit
> elit. Donec efficitur, e
> convallis quam, conse
> aliquam ex. Praesent |

See what I mean? It looks awful—text is cut off, we would have to swipe to the right...ugh! In stark contrast, adding one line of code can have a dramatic effect:

> meta name="viewport"
> content="width=device-width,
> initial-scale=1"
>
> Lorem ipsum dolor sit amet, consectetur
> adipiscing elit. Donec efficitur, elit vel auctor
> tempus, nunc dui convallis quam, consequat
> convallis ipsum est aliquam ex. Praesent porta
> nibh vel justo convallis faucibus. Nunc consequat
> turpis eget odio ornare, et molestie diam laoreet.
> Cras ullamcorper faucibus quam porta
> scelerisque. Proin finibus erat at risus laoreet
> suscipit et a neque. Nullam eu porta elit. Duis
> fermentum in lacus vel maximus. Donec vitae
> blandit nisl.

Our example uses the Google Chrome set to emulate an iPhone 6 Plus. The code needed to restore sanity to our example can be added to the <head> of our code:

```
<meta name="viewport" content="width=device-width, initial-scale=1">
```

Once set, we can immediately see the difference. Granted, our demo isn't going to win any style awards, but then it wasn't the aim! It does, however, show that the text has been reduced in size to fit the screen, we have a proper border around the text—it all looks more pleasing as a display.

 To see what happens in action, try running the `viewport.html` demo from the code download that accompanies this book; you will need to run it in device/responsive mode for your browser; remove line 5, and re-add it back in to see the difference.

The content property in this directive supports using any one of a number of different values:

Property	Description
width	The width of the virtual viewport of the device.
device-width	The physical width of the device's screen.
height	The height of the virtual viewport of the device.
device-height	The physical height of the device's screen.
initial-scale	The initial zoom when visiting the page; setting 1.0 does not zoom.
minimum-scale	The minimum amount the visitor can zoom on the page; setting 1.0 does not zoom.
maximum-scale	The maximum amount the visitor can zoom on the page; setting 1.0 does not zoom.
user-scalable	Allows the device to zoom in and out (yes) or remain fixed (no).

Current versions of MS Edge don't play so well with viewport tags; it is worth noting that `@-ms-viewport` needs to be specified in code to ensure our viewport widths behave in the same way as other browsers.

Balancing viewport against experience

You will notice that I italicized the word experience at the start of this section—the key point here is that in responsive design, the experience does not have to be identical across all devices; it must be useful though, and allow our visitors to interact with us as an organization. In other words, if we worked for a theater, we might limit our mobile offer to simply booking tickets, and let the main desktop site manage everything else.

This is perfectly valid; while limiting a site, mobile ticketing might be considered by some as very restrictive. The concept is still technically sound, as long as the user experience is acceptable.

It's worth noting that we could have set a specific width using `width=<value>`. This is great if we need a certain width to display our content; if the orientation changes from portrait (320px) to landscape (360px) for example, then the viewport's content will be automatically scaled up and down to reflect these changes. If, however, we had set a device-width as a maximum, this implies that no scaling is need and that the browser should adjust the content within it to fit.

Considering viewport units

A key part of responsive design is to make the move away from using pixel values to working with em or rem units. In our examples (and the viewport demo from earlier in this chapter), we used both pixel and rem units. Although this works well, we still have a dependency on parent elements. Instead, we should consider using an alternative for working with viewports. They are:

- **vw**: viewport width
- **vh**: viewport height
- **vmax**: maximum of the viewport's height and width
- **vmin**: minimum of the viewport's height and width

As a unit of measure, these equate to 1% of the viewport area that has been set; the beauty though is that they remove any dependency elements, and are calculated based on the current viewport size. Browser support for them is currently very good:

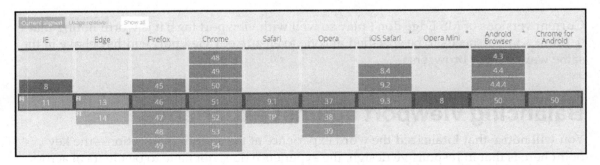

Source: `http://caniuse.com/#search=vh`

Leaving aside the slight quirks with more recent versions of Internet Explorer, this is a useful option that combines the ease of units, with the flexibility of using percentages, in our designs.

Let's move on—we've introduced flexible grids and explored how setting a viewport is critical to displaying content correctly. It's time we moved on and explore some of the benefits of incorporating a grid system into our layout, and dive into the internals of how they work as a principle in responsive design.

Exploring the benefits of flexible grid layouts

Now that we've been introduced to grid layouts as a tenet of responsive design, it's a good opportunity to explore why we should use them. Creating a layout from scratch can be time consuming and needs lots of testing; there are some real benefits from using a grid layout:

- **Grids make for a simpler design**: Instead of trying to develop the proverbial wheel, we can focus on providing the content instead; the infrastructure will have already been tested by the developer and other users.
- **They provide for a visually appealing design**: Many people prefer content to be displayed in columns, so grid layouts make good use of this concept to help organize content on the page.
- **Grids can of course adapt to different size viewports**: The system they use makes it easier to display a single codebase on multiple devices, which reduces the effort required for developers to maintain and webmasters to manage.
- **Grids help with the display of adverts**: Google has been known to favor sites which display genuine content and not those where it believes the sole purpose of the site is for ad generation; we can use the grid to define specific areas for adverts, without getting in the way of natural content.

All in all, it makes sense to familiarize ourselves with grid layouts; the temptation is of course to use an existing library. There is nothing wrong with this, but to really get the benefit out of using them, it's good to understand some of the basics around the mechanics of grid layouts and how this can help with the construction of our site.

Let's take a quick look first at how we would calculate the widths of each element, an important part of creating any grid layout.

Understanding the mechanics of grid layouts

So far, we explored one of the key critical elements of responsive design, in the form of how we would set our available screen estate (or viewport)—as someone once said, *it's time...*

Absolutely—it's time we cracked on and explored how grids operate! The trick behind grids is nothing special; it boils down to the use of a single formula to help define the proportions of each element used in our layouts:

target ÷ context = result

Let's imagine that we have a layout with two columns, and that the container (or context) is 960px wide (I will use pixel values purely to illustrate the maths involved).

To create our layout, we will make use of the Golden Ratio that we touched on in Chapter 1, *Introducing Responsive Web Design*; to recap, we use the ratio of 1.618 to every 1 pixel. So, if our layout is 960px wide, we multiply 960 x 0.618 (the difference)—this gives 593px (rounded down to the nearest integer). We then simply subtract 593 from 960, to arrive at 367px for our side column. Easy, when you know how...!

At this stage, we can convert these to percentages; 593px becomes 61.77%, and the side bar will be 38.23%. Let's translate this into some sample CSS, with values rounded to 2 decimal places:

```
section, aside {
    margin: 1.00%;      /*  10px ÷ 960px = 0.010416 */
}

section {
    float: left;
    width: 61.77%;      /* 593px ÷ 960px = 0.617708 */
}

aside {
    float: right;
    width: 38.23%;      /* 367px ÷ 960px = 0.382291 */
}
```

Here, our target is the `aside` (or sub-element), with context as the container; in this case, we've set it to 960px. The section forms a second target; in both cases, we've divided the target by the context to arrive at our result. As our result figures need to be expressed as percentages, we can simply multiply each by 100 to get the figures we need.

The observant among you will note the presence of margin: 1.00%. We must allow sufficient space for our margin, so the resulting figures will need to change. We'll keep the section width at 61.77%, so our margin will need to drop down to 34.23%, to retain a full width of 100% (this allows for the two margins each side of the two sub-elements).

If we carried this through to its conclusion, we could end up with something akin to this screenshot, as an example layout:

Okay, let's move on. I feel it's time for a demo! Before we get stuck into writing code, there are a few pointers we should take a quick look at:

- Although we've only scraped the surface of how grid layouts work, there is a lot more we can do; it will all depend on how many columns your site needs, whether the columns should be equal in width, or be merged with others, how big the container will be, and so on.
- There are dozens of grid layout frameworks available online. Before getting into designing and creating your own from scratch, take a look at what is available; it will save you a lot of time!
- Keep it simple; don't try to overcomplicate your layout. You may read stories of developers extolling the virtues of flexbox, or that you must use JavaScript or jQuery in some form or other; for a simple layout, it isn't necessary. Yes, we might use properties such as box sizing, but flexbox-based grid systems can become overinflated with CSS.

With this in mind, it's time we got stuck into a demo. Before we do though, there is something we need to cover, as it will become a recurring theme throughout this book:

We will avoid the use of JavaScript or downloading libraries in order to create our demos. Yes, you heard right. We're going to attempt to use nothing more than plain HTML5 or CSS3 to construct our responsive elements!

The reason for this is simple—I maintain that we've become lazy as developers, and that sometimes it is good to go back to basics and really appreciate that sometimes simple is better. You may hear of singers who want to get back to their roots or where they started from; we're simply applying the same principle to our responsive development. It does mean that we can't always use the most feature-rich, or latest version, but that isn't always a bad thing, right?

Implementing a prebuilt grid layout

We've touched on the basics of creating grids; these can be really time consuming to create from scratch, so with so many already available online, it makes better sense to use a prebuilt version unless your requirements are such that you can't find one that works for you! It is worth spending time researching what is available, as no two grids are the same.

As an example of what is available and to prove that we don't need all the bells and whistles that grids can offer, let's take a look at an example grid, in the form of Gridism. We can see an example of how our next demo looks like when completed, in this screenshot:

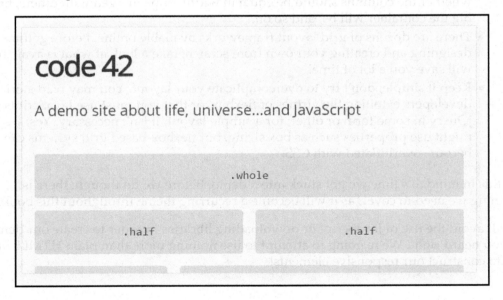

Although this library has been around for two to three years, its simplicity proves that we don't need to implement a complex solution in order to create the basis for a simple layout. The flexbox attribute in CSS is perfect for creating grids, but its flexibility adds a layer of complexity that isn't needed; instead, we'll make use of the `box-sizing` attribute, which will work just as well.

Created by Cody Chapple, it doesn't make use of flexbox (of which more, anon), but does make use of box-sizing as an attribute in the grid. The library can be downloaded from `http s://github.com/cobyism/gridism/blob/master/gridism.css` (or installed using Bower), but as it consists of one file only, we can simply copy the contents to a text file and save it that way (and still keep to our earlier aim of not downloading content).

 The demo will use the original example from the Gridism site, but the CSS has been reworked to bring it up to date and remove some unnecessary code. For ease of convenience, we will assume use of Google Chrome throughout this demo.

Let's make a start:

1. From the code download that accompanies this book, go ahead and download a copy of `gridism.html`, along with `normalize.css`, `gridism.css`, and `style.css`. Save the HTML markup at the root of our project area, and the two CSS files within the CSS subfolder.

2. Try running `gridism.html` in a browser, then enable its device or responsive mode (by pressing *Ctrl + Shift + I* then *Ctrl + Shift + M*). We should see something akin to the screenshot shown at the beginning of this exercise.

3. The screenshot at the start of this section was taken in Google Chrome, set to emulate an iPhone 6 Plus in landscape mode. Now use the orientation tool in Chrome:

4. To change the orientation to portrait:

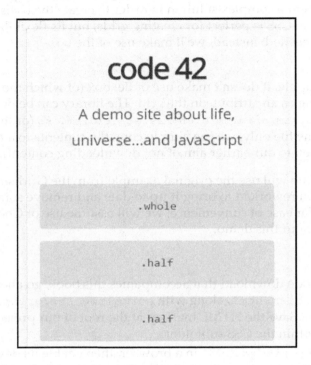

Notice how the grid has automatically realigned itself? The trick here is not in the `style.css` file, but within `gridism.css`; if we open it in a text editor and look for this block of code, on or around lines 50-61, it will look like this:

```
47   /* Width classes also have shorthand versions numbered as fractions
48    * For example: for a grid unit 1/3 (one third) of the parent width,
49    * simply apply class="w-1-3" to the element. */
50   .grid .whole,         .grid .w-1-1 { width: 100%; }
51   .grid .half,          .grid .w-1-2 { width: 50%; }
52   .grid .one-third,     .grid .w-1-3 { width: 33.3332%; }
53   .grid .two-thirds,    .grid .w-2-3 { width: 66.6665%; }
54   .grid .one-quarter,   .grid .w-1-4 { width: 25%; }
55   .grid .three-quarters, .grid .w-3-4 { width: 75%; }
56   .grid .one-fifth,     .grid .w-1-5 { width: 20%; }
57   .grid .two-fifths,    .grid .w-2-5 { width: 40%; }
58   .grid .three-fifths,  .grid .w-3-5 { width: 60%; }
59   .grid .four-fifths,   .grid .w-4-5 { width: 80%; }
60   .grid .golden-small,  .grid .w-g-s { width: 38.2716%; } /* Golden section: smaller piece */
61   .grid .golden-large,  .grid .w-g-1 { width: 61.7283%; } /* Golden section: larger piece */
```

We can see that the library makes good use of percentage values to assign a width to each block. The real crux of this is not in the widths set, but the size of our container; for gridism, this is set to 978px by default. So, for example, if we were to set a cell width of .one-third, we would want 33.3332% of 736px, or 245.33px. We then ensure all grid cells have the right dimensions by applying the box-sizing attribute to each of our grid cells.

See how easy that was? In place of having to work out percentages, we simply specify the name of the column type we need, depending on how wide we need it to be:

Hold on a moment. How come the screenshot shows 215.33, and not 245.33, as the calculation indicated it should be?

Aha, this is just something we need to be mindful of; when working with a grid system like Gridism, the calculations are based on the full width of our viewport. Any padding required will be included within the width calculations of our column, so we may need a slightly larger column then we anticipate! It goes to show that even though our grid system doesn't have all of the mod-cons of current systems, we can still produce a useable grid, as long as we plan it carefully.

Okay, let's move on. We talked in passing about the fact that many grids use flexbox to help control their appearance; this is a great option to use, but can require setting a lot of additional properties that would otherwise be unnecessary for simple layouts. With careful planning, there is every possibility that we can avoid using it, but if we're working on a complex layout with lots of different elements, then there will be occasions when using it will avoid a lot of heartache! With this in mind, let's take a quick look at the basics of how it works in more detail.

Exploring the use of flexbox

So, what is flexbox?

It's a module that has been designed to provide a more efficient way to layout and distribute space around items in a container, particularly if their sizes are not yet known. We can set a number of properties to ensure that each item best uses the available space around it, even if its size changes.

At the time of writing, this is a W3C Candidate Recommendation; this means that it is effectively on the last call before becoming a browser standard in late 2016. This should be something of a formality though, as most browsers already support it as a standard:

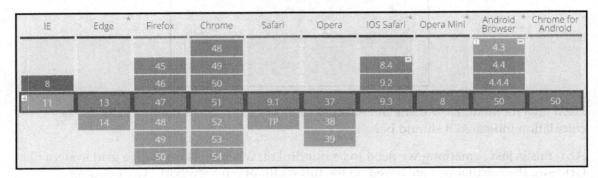

IE	Edge	Firefox	Chrome	Safari	Opera	iOS Safari	Opera Mini	Android Browser	Chrome for Android
			48					4.3	
	45	49			8.4		4.4		
8		46	50			9.2		4.4.4	
11	13	47	51	9.1	37	9.3	8	50	50
	14	48	52	TP	38				
		49	53		39				
		50	54						

Source: `http://caniuse.com/#search=flexbox`

To fully understand how it all works is outside the scope of this book, but to help get started, we can run a quick demo, and explore some of the main features:

1. From the code download that accompanies this book, go ahead and extract copies of `flexbox.html` and `flexbox.css`; store the HTML markup at the root of our project area, and the CSS style sheet in the `css` subfolder of our project area.

2. Try previewing `flexbox.html` in a browser. For this, we will need to enable the browser's responsive mode (or device mode, depending on browser); if all is well, we should see something akin to this screenshot:

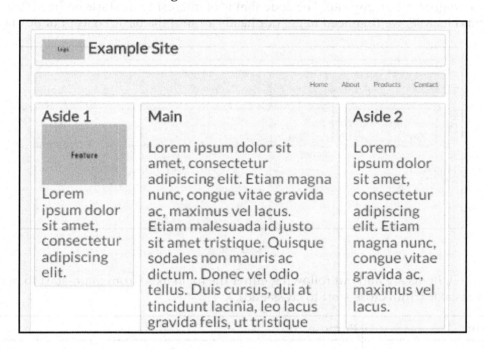

The demo is based on a pen created by Irina Kramer, which is available at `https://codepen.io/irinakramer/pen/jcLlp`; for the purposes of our demo, we focus on the example layout taken from that pen.

At first glance, this demo looks very straightforward. It could certainly use some help in the color department, but that's not what is of interest to us at the moment. If we dig deeper into the code, we can see that flexbox has been incorporated in various places; let's explore its use in more detail.

Taking a closer look

Taking a closer look at our code, we will find that a large part of it uses standard attributes, which we might find on any site. The code that is of interest to us starts on line 50; to understand its role, we first need to get our heads around the basic concept of flex layouts:

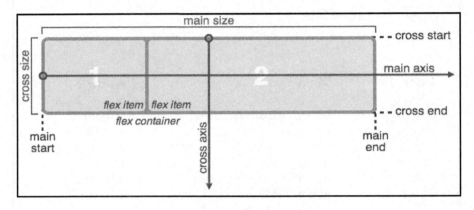

Source: W3C

In a nutshell, items are laid out following either the main axis (from main-start to main-end) or the cross axis (from cross-start to cross-end):

Property	Purpose
main axis	The primary axis along which flex items are laid out; this is dependent on the flex-direction property.
main-start | main-end	The start and end points of flex items that are placed within the container (horizontally).
main size	A flex item's width or height, whichever is in the main dimension, is the item's main size. The main size property can be the item's height or width size.
cross axis	The axis perpendicular to the main axis. Its direction depends on the main axis direction.
cross-start | cross-end	Start and end points for flex lines that are filled with items and placed into the container (vertically).
cross size	This is the width or height of a flex item, whichever is in the cross dimension.

With this in mind, let's explore some of the flexbox terms that have been used in our code; the initial few styles are standard rules that could apply to any site. The code of interest to us starts on line 29.

If we scroll down to that line, we are met with this:

```
50  /*Basic Grid Styles*/
51  .Grid {
52    display: flex;
53    flex-flow: row;
54    flex-wrap: wrap;
55  }
56
57  .Grid-cell {
58    flex: 1;
59  }
```

Our first attribute, `display: flex`, defines the container which contains the flex items; here, we're setting it to show items in rows, and to wrap from left to right. If we had a number of columns in our layout, and by this I mean more than just two or three, then we might use `align-items` and `justify-content` to ensure that each column was evenly spread throughout the row, irrespective of the width of each column.

With the `.grid` defined, we need to style our grid-cells, or the containers where we host our content. There are several properties we can apply; the one we've used is `flex`, which is shorthand for `flex-grow`, `flex-shrink`, and `flex-basis`. In our case, it is recommended that the shorthand version be used, as this will set the other values automatically; we've set `flex-grow` to 1, which indicates how much it should grow, in relation to other flexible items in the same container.

The next property of interest is in the `.nav` rule. Here, we've used flex-flow again, but this time we also justify-content; the latter controls how items are packed on each row (in this case, toward the end of the line):

```
67  .nav {
68    list-style: none;
69    background: rgba(102, 51, 255, 0.1);
70    margin: 0 0 1em;
71    border: 1px solid #33cccc;
72    border-radius: 3px;
73    display: flex;
74    flex-flow: row wrap;
75    justify-content: flex-end;
76  }
```

Our last block of code of particular interest is this section, within the large screen media query:

```
149    .Grid--Holy-grail .aside-1 {
150      order: 1;
151    }
152
153    .Grid--Holy-grail .main {
154      order: 2;
155    }
```

The order property simply specifies the order of each item in our flex container; in this case, we have `.aside-1` and `.aside-2` in position 1 and 2 respectively (not in shot), with the `.main` in the middle at position 2.

 There are a lot more properties we can set, depending on our requirements. Take a look at the source code on the original pen. There are plenty of reference sources about flexbox available online—as a start, have a look at Chris Coyier's guide, available at `http://bit.ly/1xEYMhF`.

Let's move on. We've explored some examples of what is possible now, but there is at least one downside with using flexbox. The technology works very well, but can add a fair amount of code and complexity when implementing in a site.

It's time to look for something simpler to use, which doesn't require quite the same effort to implement; enter CSS grid templates! This is still an early technology, with minimal browser support, but is already easier to implement. Let's dive in and take a look in more detail.

Visiting the future

Imagine that we have flexbox as a technique for creating grid layouts, but its design is meant for simpler, one-dimensional layouts; it doesn't work so well if the layout is complicated! Is there an answer, something better, that is designed for the job?

Fortunately there is; I am of course referring to a relatively new technology, named CSS Grid Layout. Support for this is minimal for now, but this is likely to change. In a nutshell, it provides a simpler way to create grids in a browser, without the plethora of options we saw with flexbox.

The downside of using CSS Grid Layout as a technology is that support for it has yet to hit mainstream; it is supported in IE11/Edge, but only under the −ms− prefix. Opera, Firefox, and Chrome offer support, but all require a flag to be enabled to view the results:

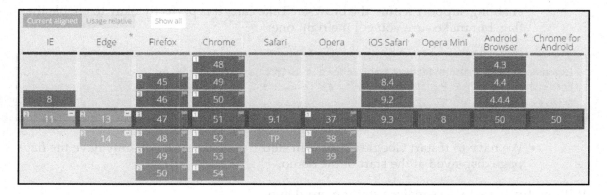

IE	Edge	Firefox	Chrome	Safari	Opera	iOS Safari	Opera Mini	Android Browser	Chrome for Android
			48					4.3	
		45	49			8.4		4.4	
8		46	50			9.2		4.4.4	
11	13	47	51	9.1	37	9.3	8	50	50
	14	48	52	TP	38				
		49	53		39				
		50	54						

Source: CanIUse.com

Leaving aside the concerns about support for a moment, it is easy to see why CSS Grid Layout will take off as a technique. The whole concept has been designed to simplify how we reference cells, rows, and columns; if we compare with flexbox, it is more straightforward to apply styles using CSS Grid Layout than with flexbox.

 If you would like to learn more about CSS Grid Layout, then have a look online. This article by Chris House explains it well: http://bit.ly/2bMGl Dp.

To see how it compares, let's dive in and build a simple demo to illustrate some images in a grid layout.

Implementing a basic gallery grid

For our next demo, we're going to make use of an example created by the developer Rachel Andrew, at http://codepen.io/rachelandrew/full/LGpONE/; we'll be replacing the images with ones from Flickr, depicting pictures of my favorite European town, Bruges. No, it's not to do with the lace, before you ask: good food, fine wine, great atmosphere, stunning chocolates for sale…what more could you ask for, I wonder?

But I digress. Before we get into creating our code, there are a couple of points we must bear in mind:

- This demo is cutting edge, it won't work in all browsers, and for some, it requires enabling support within the browser. Take care, it is perfectly okay to enable the flag, but make sure you get the right one:

Experimental Web Platform features Mac, Windows, Linux, Chrome OS, Android
Enables experimental Web Platform features that are in development. #enable-experimental-web-platform-features
Disable

- We have to restart Google Chrome in step 1, so make sure you only have the flags page displayed at the start of the demo.

Without further ado, let's make a start on our demo:

1. We'll begin by enabling support in Google Chrome for CSS Grid Layout. To do so, browse to `chrome://flags` and search for **Experimental Web Platform features**. Click on the enable button to activate it, then hit the blue **Relaunch Now** button at the bottom of the page to relaunch Google Chrome.
2. With support enabled, go ahead and extract a copy of `gridtemplate.html` from the code download that accompanies this book; save it to the root of our project area.
3. In a new text file, add the following styles. We'll go through them in blocks, beginning with some initial styling for our images and labels:

```
body {
    font-family: helvetica neue, sans-serif;
}

img {
    max-width: 100%;
    border-radius: 10px;
}
```

4. Next up comes the rules needed to set our container; note that the only style used that relates to our grid is `box-sizing`, which we set to `border-box`:

```
.wrapper {
    list-style: none;
    margin: 0;
    padding: 0;
```

```
}

.wrapper li {
  box-sizing: border-box;
  padding: 1em;
  min-width: 1%;
}
```

5. The real magic starts to happen in a set of media queries; we begin with assigning wrapper as our grid container, then set the column and row layout of our grid:

```
@media screen and (min-width: 500px) {
  .wrapper {
    display: grid;
    grid-template-columns: 1fr 1fr;
  }

  .wrapper li:nth-child(1) {
    grid-column: 1 / 3;
  }
}
```

6. In our second query, we set individual styles for our grid wrapper and list items, this time for 640px or greater:

```
@media screen and (min-width: 640px) {
  .wrapper {
    grid-template-columns: 1fr 1fr 1fr;
  }

  .wrapper li:nth-child(1) {
    grid-column: 2;
    grid-row: 1 / 3;
  }

  .wrapper li:nth-child(2) {
    grid-column: 3;
    grid-row: 2;
  }

  .wrapper li:nth-child(3) {
    grid-column: 1;
    grid-row: 1;
  }

  .wrapper li:nth-child(4) {
    grid-column: 3;
    grid-row: 1;
```

```
    }
    .wrapper li:nth-child(5) {
      grid-column: 1;
      grid-row: 2;
    }
  }
```

7. Save the file as `gridtemplate.css`, within the `css` subfolder of our project area.

8. Try previewing the results in a browser; if all is well, we should see results similar to this screenshot:

Rozenhoedkaai at night, Bruges

Tourist store - Jackie Bernelas

Canal boat cruise - Jason Connolly

Architecture in Bruges - Frederic Giet

Bruges - Wolfgang Staudt

Okay, granted. It's probably not what you might expect in terms of styling, but this demo isn't about making it look pretty, but the basic grid effect. There are nonetheless some important concepts that are good to understand, so let's dive in and explore what took place in our demo in more detail.

Exploring what happened

Earlier in this chapter, we explored how flexbox can be used to create a grid layout; if we were to compare CSS styling, it is easy to see that on balance, we need to provide more styling when using flexbox than using CSS Grid Layout.

The only styling attribute that we've used in our core styles is `box-sizing`, which we set to `border-box`. Nothing else has been used at this point—all of our CSS Grid Layout styles have been set within two media queries.

Our first media query sets the `.wrapper` class as our grid container. Note that we've only need to set it once, as it will cascade through to larger viewports that are `500px` or greater in size.

Once the grid container is assigned, we then specify the grid columns for our template – the `1fr` value assigned represents the fraction of free white space in the grid around each cell's content (hence the `fr` unit). We then finish up by specifying `grid-row` or `grid-column` in both media queries – these values define a grid item's location within the grid; these two terms are shorthand for `grid-row-start`, `grid-row-end`, `grid-column-start` and `grid-column-end` respectively.

 For a more detailed explanation of how these terms are used in creating grids, refer to the Mozilla Developer Network articles available at `https://developer.mozilla.org/en-US/docs/Web/CSS/CSS_Grid_Layout`.

Taking it further

Learning a new technology is like putting on new clothes; at some point, we will outgrow those clothes, or they no longer present the appeal that attracted us to them at the time of purchase.

It's at times like this we need to progress onto something more advanced or with additional functionality, otherwise our development will come to a standstill! Thankfully, there are literally dozens of options available online that we can explore—one might be forgiven for thinking that there are too many and where does one start?

A great starting point is a responsive framework such as Bootstrap or Unsemantic; these have been made to improve the usability and help speed up the process of development. These frameworks were introduced with the aim of providing a grid or foundation for rapid prototyping of the various mobile functionalities, layouts which allow the designers and developers to better make use of their development time.

This is just one part of what is available to help you along, let's briefly cover a few ideas that might serve as somewhere to start:

- **Bootstrap** is downloadable from `http://getbootstrap.com/`, this veteran grid system was first created by Facebook, before becoming a standalone product in its own right.
- If you want to explore something that is more than just a framework, then **Responsive Grid System** might be an option; it's available from `http://www.responsivegridsystem.com/`, with a SASS version available for those who use that CSS preprocessor.
- Instead of simply downloading a framework, how about generating one online? For this, try **Responsify.it** (`http://responsify.it`) and Gridpak.com (`http://gridpak.com`) as possible contenders.
- We used a minimal Grid system earlier in the form of Gridfy, there are others available, if this one is not to your liking. As an example, try Gridly, which can be downloaded from `http://ionicabizau.github.io/gridly/example/`.
- It's worth noting that not every Grid system is available as a standalone—some form part of a component library. A good example is **Formstone**; its grid system is available from `https://formstone.it/components/grid/`. For those of you who use the Less CSS preprocessor, this grid comes with a version that can be used with this tool.
- Staying with the theme of component libraries, why not have a look at **Metro UI**? This library, available from `http://metroui.org.ua/grid.html`, even has backing from Microsoft; it does require jQuery though!
- Some of you might have heard of the 960.gs grid system, which was available a few years ago – it has been replaced by **Unsemantic**, which is available from `http://unsemantic.com/`.
- We covered the use of flexbox as a technology for creating grid-based layouts; as a start point, why not have a look at the PureCSS library? This is available at `http://purecss.io`; it's a good example of using flexbox to produce clean layouts without too much fuss.

As developers, this is one area of responsive design where we are spoilt for choice; the great thing about open source software is that if a framework we choose isn't right, then we can always try another! To help us make the decision, there are a few questions we can ask ourselves:

- Do you need a version that works with a CSS preprocessor? Although preprocessed CSS is a superset of standard CSS, there are grid systems available that are specifically built from a preprocessing technology such as SASS or PostCSS. This is easier than trying to convert finished CSS into something that can be compiled by our processor.

- How complex is your site? Is it a single page *calling card* affair, or something substantially more complex? There is clearly no point in burdening a simple site with a complex grid arrangement; equally if we're building a complex site, then our chosen grid system must be up to par.
- Is browser support an issue? If we can forgo support for some of the older browsers (and particularly below IE8), then choosing a CSS-only option is preferable to one dependent on using jQuery. The same principle applies if we already have to use more than just the occasional external resource. There is no need to add in a plugin if using CSS is sufficient.
- Does your site need to make use of UI components which need to be styled using a themed library? If so, check the library; it may already have a grid system built in that we can use.

The key here is that we shouldn't simply choose the first available option to us, but carefully consider what is available and pick something that satisfies our requirements where possible. Any styling can of course be overridden—the trick here is to choose the right one, so that overriding is minimal or not required for our site.

Summary

Constructing the layout grid for any site is key critical to its success; traditionally, we may have done this first, but in the world of responsive design, content comes first! Throughout the course of this chapter, we've covered a few topics to help get you started, so let's take a moment to recap what we have learned.

We kicked off with an introduction to flexible grid layouts, with a mention that we may have to change our design process to facilitate creating responsive grids. We then moved onto to explore the different types of layout we can use, and how responsive layouts compare to these different types.

Next up, we began on the most important part of our layout—setting the available viewport; this controls how much is visible at any one point. We covered the need to set a viewport directive in our code, so that content is correctly displayed; we examined how not providing the directive can have a negative impact on the appearance of our content! In addition, we covered some of the additional properties and units of value we can use, along with balancing the viewport size against user experience.

We then moved onto exploring the benefits of flexible grid layouts, before taking a look at how they work in more detail; we then created a simple demo using a prebuilt grid system available from the Internet.

Moving on, we then took a look at using flexbox as a technology; we explored it through a simple demo, before dissecting some of the issues with using flexbox. We then saw how a replacement is in the works. We rounded out the chapter with a demo to explore how it can be activated today, and that it is simpler to develop solutions for it once it becomes a mainstream standard.

Now that we have our layout in place, it's time to move on. We need to start adding content! It's assumed that text would be added by default, but what about media? How do we make it responsive? We'll answer these questions, and more, in the next chapter, when we take a look at adding responsive media to our pages.

3
Adding Responsive Media

A picture paints a thousand words…

A key element of any website is a visual content; after all, text will become very repetitive and dull, without adding some form of color!

Adding media not only gives color to a site, but can serve as a vital tool to show potential customers what a product looks like or how we should use it. In fact, sales can go up based purely on being able to see a product being demonstrated. With the advent of mobile devices, it is more important that we not only add media, but also ensure it works well on a range of different devices.

Throughout the course of this chapter, we will explore different ways of adding media to our pages, and see how easy it is to make it respond to any changes in available screen size. In this chapter, we will cover the following topics:

- Understanding the basics of adding images using `<picture>`
- Exploring alternatives to adding images
- Making video and audio content responsive
- Adjusting text to fit automatically on the screen

Curious? Let's get cracking!

Making media responsive

Our journey through the basics of adding responsive capabilities to a site has so far touched on how we make our layouts respond automatically to changes; it's time for us to do the same to media!

If your first thought is that we need lots of additional functionality to make media responsive, then I am sorry to disappoint; it's much easier, and requires zero additional software to do it! Yes, all we need is just a text editor and a browser; I'll be using my favorite editor, Sublime Text, but you can use whatever works for you.

Over the course of this chapter, we will take a look in turn at images, videos, audio, and text, and we'll see how with some simple changes, we can make each of them responsive. Let's kick off our journey, first with a look at making image content responsive.

Creating fluid images

It is often said that *images speak a thousand words*. We can express a lot more with media than we can using words. This is particularly true for websites selling products; a clear, crisp image clearly paints a better picture than a poor quality one!

When constructing responsive sites, we need our images to adjust in size automatically. To see why this is important, go ahead and extract `coffee.html` from a copy of the code download that accompanies this book and run it in a browser. Try resizing the window. We should see something akin to this:

It doesn't look great, does it? Leaving aside my predilection for nature's finest bean drink, we can't have images that don't resize properly, so let's take a look at what is involved to make this happen:

1. Go ahead and extract a copy of `coffee.html` and save it to our project area.

2. We also need our image—this is in the `img` folder; save a copy to the `img` folder in our project area.

3. In a new text file, add the following code, saving it as `coffee.css`:

```
img {
    max-width: 100%;
    height: auto;
}
```

4. Revert to `coffee.html`. You will see line 6 is currently commented out; remove the comment tags.

5. Save the file, then preview it in a browser. If all is well, we will still see the same image as before, but this time try resizing it.

This time around, our image grows or shrinks automatically, depending on the size of our browser window:

Although our image does indeed fit better, there are a couple of points we should be aware of when using this method:

- Sometimes you might see `!important` set as a property against the `height` attribute when working with responsive images; this isn't necessary, unless you're setting sizes in a site where image sizes may be overridden at a later date
- We've set `max-width` to `100%` as a minimum; you may need to set a `width` value too, to be sure that your images do not become too big and break your layout

This is an easy technique to use, although there is a downside that can trip us up—spot what it is? If we use a high-quality image, its file size will be hefty—we can't expect users of mobile devices to download it, can we?

Don't worry though – there is a great alternative that has quickly gained popularity among browsers; we can use the `<picture>` element to control what is displayed, depending on the size of the available window. Let's dive in and take a look.

Implementing the <picture> element

In a nutshell, responsive images are images that are displayed their optimal form on a page, depending on the device your website is being viewed from. This can mean several things:

- You want to show a separate image asset based on the user's physical screen size. This might be a 13.5-inch laptop or a 5-inch mobile phone screen.
- You want to show a separate image based on the resolution of the device or using the device-pixel ratio (which is the ratio of device pixels to CSS pixels).
- You want to show an image in a specified image format (WebP, for example) if the browser supports it.

Traditionally, we might have used simple scripting to achieve this, but it is at the risk of potentially downloading multiple images or none at all, if the script loads after images have loaded, or if we don't specify any image in our HTML and want the script to take care of loading images.

We clearly need a better way to manage responsive images! A relatively new tag for HTML5 is perfect for this job: `<picture>`. We can use this in one of three different ways, depending on whether we want to resize an existing image, display a larger one, or show a high-resolution version of the image. The recommended way to approach this is:

1. `srcset` attribute
2. `sizes` attribute
3. `picture` element

We'll explore all three in detail; let's start with implementing the `srcset` attribute in a standard `<img>` tag, before moving on to using the `<picture>` element.

Using the srcset attribute

A key benefit of using the `<picture>` element is using the srcset attribute to select any one of several images, based on whether we want to display higher resolution versions or different sizes of the same image in different viewports.

Support for this in browsers is very good, with only Opera Mini and up to IE11 not wanting to join the party:

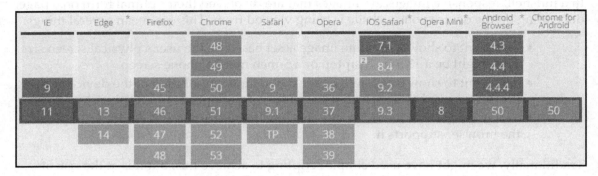

IE	Edge *	Firefox	Chrome	Safari	Opera	iOS Safari *	Opera Mini *	Android * Browser	Chrome for Android
			48			7.1		4.3	
			49			[2] 8.4		4.4	
9		45	50	9	36	9.2		4.4.4	
11	13	46	51	9.1	37	9.3	8	50	50
	14	47	52	TP	38				
		48	53		39				

Source: `http://caniuse.com/#search=srcset`

To make use of this `srcset` attribute, we need to avail ourselves of sufficient different images, then specify what should be displayed at the appropriate trigger point, as shown in this example, based on defining the `device-pixel` ratio:

```
<img src="small-image.png" srcset="small-img.png 1x, med-img.png 2x, lrg-
img.png 3x">
```

Here, the `src` attribute acts as fallback image for those browsers that do not support `srcset` (although support is now very good!). The `srcset` attribute allows us to specify different images to use, either based on the device-pixel ratio or the available viewport:

```
<img src="default.png" srcset="small.png 256w, med.jpg 511w, large.jpg
640w">
```

In this case, our fallback is `default.png`; however, if the browser being used supports `srcset`, then it will display `small.png` at `256w` or `med.png` at `511w`. If, however, we wanted to change the size and use different images based on the available viewport, then we would have to add an extra attribute—`sizes`. It's easy enough to configure, so let's pause for a moment to see what this means in practice.

Exploring the sizes attribute

When adding pictures as part of the content on a responsive site, the images may each take up 100% of the element width, but the content itself doesn't always take 100% of the width of the window! For example, we might set each image element to 100% width (so they fill their parent containers), but that the overall content on screen only fills 50% of the available screen width.

To overcome this, we need to know the URLs for the various images to use, along with the width of each image resource; we can't get this from standard markup in the page layout, as images start downloading before CSS is applied.

Instead, we can simply set suitable widths within our HTML code using the `srcset` attribute and suitable width descriptors. This is a little controversial for some, as it starts to blur the divide between HTML markup and the CSS presentation layer. This aside, let's take a look at an example of how we can set up the code:

```
<img src="img/orchid.jpg" sizes="50vw" srcset="img/orchid.jpg 200w,
img/orchid-2x.jpg 400w, img/orchid-hd.jpg 600w">
```

In this excerpt, we set a default of 50% or half of the viewport width; the browser can then select the appropriate image to display, depending on the available width.

Manipulating the HTML5 <picture> element

We've covered two key parts of making images responsive, but to bring it all together, we can use the HTML5<picture> element, which has garnered good support in most browsers:

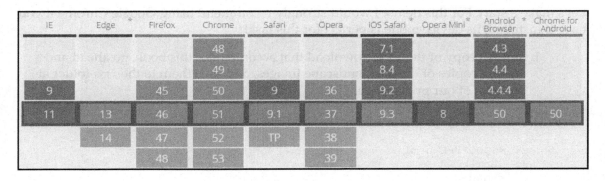

Source: `http://caniuse.com/#search=picture`

The `<picture>` element uses this syntax:

```
<picture>
   <source media="(min-width: 60rem)" sizes="(max-width: 500px) 50vw, 10vw"
   src="high-res-image-2x.png 145w ">
   <source media="(min-width: 35rem)" src="med-res-image.png">
   <source src="low-res-image.png">
   <img src="fallback-image.png" alt="Non-supported browser.">
   <p>Text to display</p>
</picture>
```

In this extract, we've tied together all of the various attributes we can use with the `<picture>` element; in this case, we've specified media queries (one of `60rem` and another of `35rem`), and that if our viewport is only 50% or less (indicated by the `50vw` value in the code), we display the normal images; if it is higher, then we display the high-definition images (as specified by using the `100vw` value).

 We will explore how this works in more detail, in *Exploring what happened*, later in this chapter.

Putting it all together

Now that we've seen all three elements in use, let's pull them together and create a simple demo that automatically adjusts which image to use, based on the available viewport. For simplicity, we will concentrate just on the image, but there is nothing stopping us from developing this further into a full-sized page!

Let's make a start. For this demo, I would strongly recommend using Google Chrome if you have it installed; its device mode is perfect for this task!

1. From a copy of the code download that accompanies this book, go ahead and extract copies of the four landscape images, and save them to the `img` folder at the root of our project area.

2. Next, fire up your text editor, and add the following code:

```
<!DOCTYPE html>
<html>
<head>
<title>Adding responsive images with the <picture> element</title>
</head>
<body>
```

```
<picture>
  <source media="(min-width: 800px)" sizes="(max-width: 1000px)
  100vw" srcset="img/high-res-image.png 738w">
  <source media="(max-width: 799px)" sizes="(max-width: 600px)
  100vw" srcset="img/med-res-image.png 738w">
  <img src="img/fallback-image.png" alt="Human">
</picture>
</body>
</html>
```

3. Save this as `pictureelement.html` at the root of our project folder.
4. Go ahead and preview the results of the file in Google Chrome (or another browser if preferred). Make sure you switch on that browser's device/responsive mode.

If all is well, we should see the image flip between two similar versions; to identify which is which, I've added the words **High Resolution Image** on one, and **Medium Resolution Image** on the other image used:

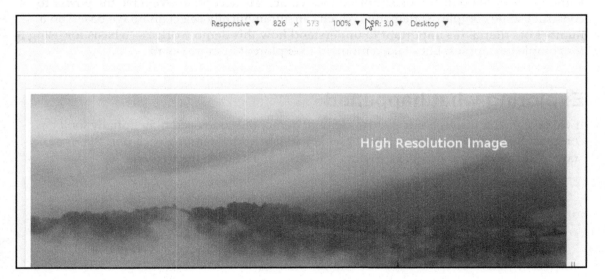

This is the same image, but this time using the medium resolution version:

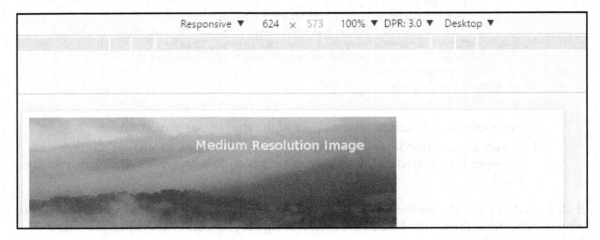

Although this demo may look simple at face value, it is deceptive. We have the power to construct some complex statements, which can automatically select an image based on a number of criteria! It's important to understand how this demo works, as a basis for using it for complex examples. Let's take a moment to explore it in more detail.

Exploring what happened

If we take a look through our picture element demo, the code used may initially look complex, but is simpler than it looks! The key to it is understanding each part the `<source>` statements and how they interact with each other. Let's tackle the first one:

```
<picture>
  <source media="(min-width: 800px)" sizes="(max-width: 1000px) 100vw"
  srcset="img/high-res-image.png 738w">
  ...
</picture>
```

In this one, we're specifying `high-res-image.png` as our source image; this will only be displayed when our browser window is showing a minimum width of `800px`. The size of the image will either go to a maximum of `1000px` or `100vw`—the latter equivalent to 100% width of the available viewport space. The `738w` against the image is just the width of the image specified in the code (1w unit is equal to 1px, so our image is 738px wide).

Moving onto the second source statement, we find it shows a similar set up, but this time the media query is limited to a maximum width of `799px`, and that the size of the image will go to `600px` or the full width of the viewport, depending on its current size:

```
<picture>
    ...
    <source media="(max-width: 799px)" sizes="(max-width: 600px) 100vw"
    srcset="img/med-res-image.png 738w">
    <img src="img/fallback-image.png" alt="Human">
</picture>
```

To finish off the `<picture>` element, we specify `fallback-image.png` as our fallback for those browsers that have yet to support this element in HTML5.

 We've only scratched the surface of what is possible with the `<picture>` element; for more details, take a look at the site maintained by the Responsive Images Community Group, hosted at `https://responsiveim ages.org/`.

Creating a real-world example

We've explored the theory behind making images responsive with a couple of useful techniques; it's time we got practical! The basis for our next demo is going to look at making a responsive map using Google Maps.

Responsive maps, I hear you ask? Surely this should come automatically, right? Well no, it doesn't, which makes its use a little awkward on mobile devices. Fortunately, we can easily fix this; the great thing about it is that it only requires a little additional CSS:

1. Let's make a start by browsing to `http://maps.google.com`, then entering the zip code of our chosen location; in this instance, I will use Packt's UK office, which is B3 2PB.

2. Click on the cog, then select **Share and embed** map, as shown in this screenshot:

3. In the dialog box that appears, switch to the Embed map tab, then copy the contents of the text field starting with `<iframe src=....`

4. In a copy of the code download that accompanies this book, extract a copy of `googlemaps.html` in your favorite text editor, and add the `<iframe>` code in between the google-maps div tags.

5. Next, add the following CSS styling to a new file, saving it as `googlemaps.css`:

```
#container { margin: 0 auto; padding: 5px; max-width: 40rem; }
.google-maps { position: relative; padding-bottom: 60%;overflow:
hidden; }
.google-maps iframe { position: absolute; top: 0; left: 0; width:
100% !important; height: 100% !important; }
```

If all is well, we will see a Google Maps image of Birmingham, with Packt's office marked accordingly:

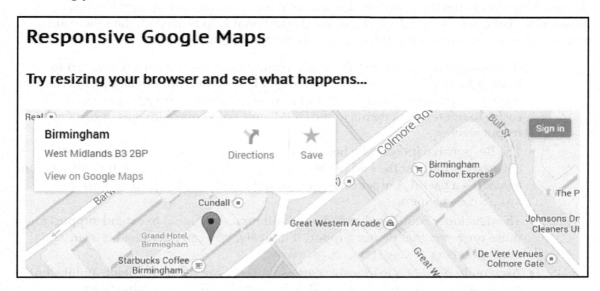

At this point, try resizing the browser window. You will see that the map resizes automatically; the CSS styling that we've added has overridden the standard styles used within Google Maps to make our map responsive and accessible from any device we care to use.

Taking things further

Throughout the course of this chapter, we've followed the principle of using just a browser and text editor to construct our code. This, of course, included not downloading anything that was core to creating our examples (save for media and content).

There will be times though when this approach is not sufficient, we may find we need to avail ourselves of additional support to get a job done. Our overriding question should always be to check that we really need it, and that we're not just being lazy! If when answering that question, we do find that need additional help is needed, then there are a number of sources you can try out, to help take things further:

- It goes without saying, but there will come a time when we need to resort to using jQuery (`http://www.jquery.com`) to help within our development. The state of responsive design is such that we should only need jQuery to make it easier to reference elements in the DOM, and not to make images or content responsive!

- The Responsive Images site hosted at `https://responsiveimages.org/`. We covered it briefly at the end of the `<picture>` demo, but it's worth pointing it out again. It's a useful compendium of material to help understand and use the `<picture>` element.

- The developer Scott Jehl created a polyfill for `<picture>`, to extend support to those browsers that do not support it natively; you can download it from `https://scottjehl.github.io/picturefill/`.

- Are you in need of a responsive carousel? There are plenty available online, but one which I've found to work well, is ResponsiveSlides, available from `http://responsiveslides.com/`. Granted, the project is a few years old, but this particular plugin keeps things nice and simple, which is very much in keeping with the theme for this book!

- A good example of where responsive capabilities are already present is in using the SVG image format. These are effectively vector-based images that we can manipulate using CSS; the key benefit though is that SVG images can automatically grow or shrink, with no loss of quality. Browser support for the format is excellent, although IE (and Edge) both have a couple of quirks that require attention when using these browsers (for more details, see `http://caniuse.com/#feat=svg`).

- Another idea to try is with responsive icons. A good example that is worth a look is the FontAwesome library, available from `http://fontawesome.io/`. These will resize equally as well. In this instance, they would be perfect for smaller images, such as credit card icons or shopping baskets on e-commerce sites.

- Taking things even further afield, how about support for the WebP image format? Yes, this is one that hasn't gained huge support yet, with it being limited to Chrome and Opera at the time of writing. However, when used with the `<picture>` element, it shows off a nice trick:

```
<picture>
    <source type="image/webp" srcset="retina-image.webp 2x,
    image.webp 1x" />
    <img srcset="retina-image.jpg 2x" src="image.jpg"
    alt="an image" />
</picture>
```

- In our example, the browser will check for WebP support, if it can support it, it will display the appropriate image in WebP format, depending on what device-pixel-ratio is supported on the device being used. If WebP isn't supported, then it will fall back to using JPEG (although this could equally have been a different format such as PNG).

There are certainly things we can do, once we've become accustomed to working with responsive images, and want to graduate away from just using HTML5 and CSS3. It is important to note though, that there are a number of projects operating online that aren't listed here.

The main reason for this is age—support for responsive images was patchy for a while, which meant a number of projects appeared to help provide support for responsive images. Support for the `<picture>` and associated elements is getting better all of the time, which reduces some of the attraction of these older projects; it is worth considering whether it is sensible to use them, or if the impact of not using them can be mitigated by changes to the user experience.

Okay, let's move on; time to get a little animated, I think! Alright, that was a terrible lead in to our next topic, given that we're going to explore making videos responsive. Over the next few pages, we'll see that although some of the same principles apply here, there are some bumps along the way, which might impact our journey.

Making video responsive

Flexible videos are somewhat more complex than images. The HTML5 `<video>` maintains its aspect ratio just like images and therefore we can apply the same CSS principle to make it responsive:

```
video {
    max-width: 100%;
    height: auto !important;
}
```

Until relatively recently, there have been issues with HTML5 video—this is mainly due to split support for the codecs required to run HTML video. The CSS required to make a HTML5 video is very straightforward, but using it directly presents a few challenges:

- Hosting video is bandwidth intensive and expensive
- Streaming requires complex hardware support in addition to video
- It is not easy to maintain a consistent look and feel across different formats and platforms

For many, a better alternative is to host the video through a third-party service such as YouTube. There is a caveat that they would be in control of your video content; if this isn't an issue, we can let them worry about bandwidth issues and providing a consistent look and feel; we just have to make it fit on the page! This requires a little more CSS styling to make it work, so let's explore what is involved.

Embedding externally hosted videos

To embed those videos, we need to use iframes, which unfortunately do not maintain aspect ratio by default; we can work around this with a CSS solution by Thierry Koblentz.

Let's for argument's sake say that we have a YouTube video, such as this one, titled *The Big Buck Bunny*, by the Blender Foundation:

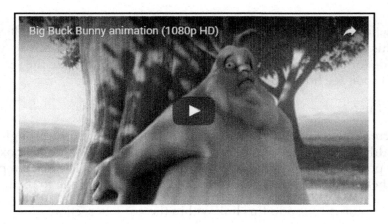

(c) Blender Foundation | www.bigbuckbunny.org

Looks okay, doesn't it? Granted, we can't immediately tell it is a video from YouTube, but this next screenshot clearly shows it is:

Hold on; that doesn't look right, does it? The screenshot was taken in Google, but set to emulate the screen estate of a Galaxy S5 mobile phone, but it clearly shows that the video is not responsive.

To see this in action, extract a copy of youtube.html from the code download that accompanies this book to our project area, then run it in a browser. Activate your browser's responsive mode (or device mode, depending on browser) and resize the screen to 360px by 640px. You will soon see how it doesn't resize well!

How do we fix this?

The trick is to create a box with a proper aspect ratio, say 4:3 or 16:9 (through zero height and bottom padding in %), and then fit the video and stretch it inside the box up to the box dimensions by positioning it absolutely with respect to the box. The bottom padding acts as the width that helps to maintain the aspect ratio. Let's alter our code to fix this issue:

1. In youtube.html, add this link within the <head> section:

    ```
    <link rel="stylesheet" type="text/css" href="css/youtube.css">
    ```

2. Further down, alter the code as shown:

    ```
    <div class="video-box-wrapper">
      <iframe width="560" height="315"
      src="https://www.youtube.com/embed/XSGBVzeBUbk" frameborder="0"
      allowfullscreen></iframe>
    </div>
    ```

3. Save the file. Switch to a new file, then add the following code and save it as youtube.css within the css subfolder of our project area:

    ```
    .video-box-wrapper {
      padding-bottom: 5.25%; height: 0; position: relative;padding-top:
      1.875rem; overflow: hidden; }

    .video-box-wrapper iframe,
    .video-box-wrapper object,
    .video-box-wrapper embed { position: absolute; left: 0; top: 0;
    width: 100%; height: 100%; }
    ```

 A word of note—setting height: 0 ensures the element is present within the DOM so that older browsers can format the inner box properly.

4. Save the file, revert back to your browser, and re-enable its responsive (or device) mode if it is not already switched on.

5. Try previewing the results now; if all is well, we should see something akin to this. It uses the same Galaxy S5 size settings, but this time zoomed in to 150% for clarity:

This looks much better! With some simple styling, we have the best of both worlds; we can let YouTube do all the heavy lifting while we concentrate on making our video available from our site on multiple devices. The CSS we used forces all of the video content to the full width of the .video-box-wrapper container, which in turn is positioned relative to its normal position. We then add 56.25% to the bottom to maintain the classic 16:9 aspect ratio and provide a little extra padding at the top so it doesn't appear to go off screen!

Question: How did we arrive at 56.25%? This is simply 9 divided by 16 (the aspect ratio), which is 0.5625 or 56.25%.

There will be occasions, though, when we have to host our own videos; this might be for controlling visibility or preventing adverts from being played, if we were to host it externally. To achieve this, we can use the now current HTML5 <video> element to render content on a page; let's take a look and see how this works in action.

Introducing the new HTML5 video element

If hosting videos on an external source is not possible, then we must host locally; for this, we can use the native HTML5 video tag, which looks something like this:

```
<video controls>
  <source src="video/bigbuckbunny.webm" type="video/webm">
  <source src="video/bigbuckbunny.mp4" type="video/mp4">
</video>
```

In the past, codec support for the HTML5 element has been split across each platform; in 2015, Firefox added support for H.264 to its browsers across all platforms, which goes a long way to rationalize support for HTML5 video. At present, support for the two formats (MP4 and WebM) is good, but not 100% across all browsers – this screenshot indicates the current state of play for desktop and mobile browsers for the MP4 format:

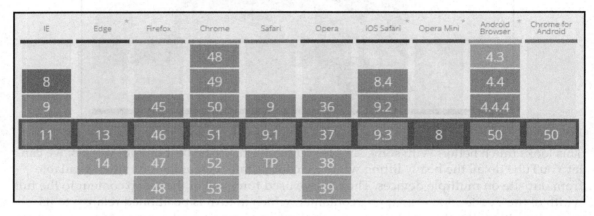

IE	Edge	Firefox	Chrome	Safari	Opera	iOS Safari	Opera Mini	Android Browser	Chrome for Android
			48					4.3	
8			49			8.4		4.4	
9		45	50	9	36	9.2		4.4.4	
11	13	46	51	9.1	37	9.3	8	50	50
	14	47	52	TP	38				
		48	53		39				

Source: CanIuse.com

In contrast, support for the WebM format is not quite so complete:

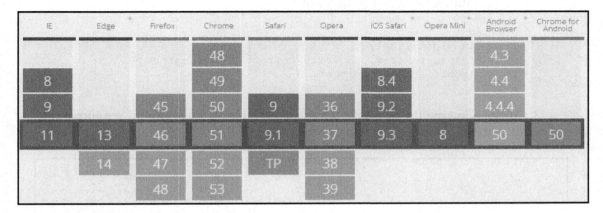

IE	Edge	Firefox	Chrome	Safari	Opera	iOS Safari	Opera Mini	Android Browser	Chrome for Android
			48					4.3	
8			49			8.4		4.4	
9		45	50	9	36	9.2		4.4.4	
11	13	46	51	9.1	37	9.3	8	50	50
	14	47	52	TP	38				
		48	53		39				

Source: CanIuse.com

In reality, the only format we need to worry about using is MP4; we can use WebM format if desired. If we do so, then it must come first in the `<source>` list; otherwise, the browser will pick the first available supported format (in this case, MP4) and not use WebM!

> Before continuing, I would strongly recommend making sure you have Google Chrome or Firefox installed – WebM video will work in IE9 or above, but not without adding codec support for the format!

Now that we've been introduced, let's move on and put it into practice, with a simple demo to illustrate how the `<video>` element works in action.

Embedding HTML5 video content

If our requirements are such that we have to host a video ourselves, then implementing it using the HTML5 standard tags is very easy; it consists of setting any number of different sources within the `<video>` tags so that we can play the same video using the supported format for that browser. Let's dive in and take a look at how we do it:

1. We'll start by extracting copies of the following, from the code download that accompanies this book – the `video` folder and `html5video.html`. Save them to the root of our project folder.

2. In a new file, go ahead and add these styles; save the file as `html5video.css` in the `css` subfolder of our project area:

```
video {
    max-width: 100%;
    /* just in case, to force correct aspect ratio */
    height: auto !important;
}
```

3. Try previewing the results in a browser. If all is well, we should see something akin to this (screenshot taken from Chrome):

The result looks perfect—the question is, which version of our video is being used? One way to find out is to right-click on the video, while it is still playing, then click on **Save video as...**. If all is well, we should see a **Save As** dialog box open, ready to save the WebM format if we're using FireFox, Chrome, or Opera; otherwise it will be MP4 (if using IE).

Exploring what happened

The real question, though, is not so much how does it all work, but if it is responsive?

The answer is yes; our use of the HTML5`<video>` tags mean that we can select any number of different video formats to use; the browser will simply choose the first available that it is able to play. The order is critical though:

```
<video controls>
    <source src="video/bigbuckbunny.webm" type="video/webm">
    <source src="video/bigbuckbunny.mp4" type="video/mp4">
</video>
```

If we were to swap it around so that MP4 is first, then WebM will be ignored for almost all browsers, as MP4 can be played in almost all of the browsers!

The real magic lies not in the use of a specific video format, but in the CSS rule we've created:

```
video {
    max-width: 100%;
    /* just in case, to force correct aspect ratio */
    height: auto !important;
}
```

Our use of percentage values means that it will automatically scale up or down when our window is resized; the maximum size of the video is constrained by the video's dimensions, not other elements on screen. Of course, we may decide to host the video within a parent container; the video will fill that container, but the parent may only stretch over part of the site.

Building a practical example

If you spend any time on the Internet, it's possible you've come across sites where the developer hasn't used images as a background, but *video*.

This isn't entirely new as a concept; it's been around for a couple of years now. If done with care, it can work very well. It's a perfect candidate for making full-size video as a responsive background. The great thing about it is that we can make it responsive using pure CSS. That's right, no need for any JavaScript.

For our next demo, we'll take a break from creating content. This time around, we'll run the demo from the code download that accompanies this book, and take a look at the code in more detail later in the demo. We'll be using videos from the Big Buck Bunny project, created by the Blender Foundation as our background; over this, we'll overlay a simple block of sample text, generated using the Lorem Ipsum generator.

To see this in action, go ahead and run the `fullscreen .html` demo from a copy of the code download that accompanies this book. If all is well, you will see the video play behind a simple `<div>` with text:

If we take a look at our code in more detail, we can see the video element in use; it's been set to autoplay, with sound muted and a poster (or placeholder) image set. The real magic, though, lies in the CSS styling, so let's explore this in more detail.

Exploring what happened

The trick that makes our video work is in this code. We need to set two media queries with 16:9 aspect ratio (one as a min-aspect-ratio, another as the max) so that our video displays correctly on the screen:

```
60  @media (max-width: 47.9375rem) {
61      .fullscreen {
62          background: url('../img/videoframe.jpg') center center / cover no-repeat;
63      }
64
65      .fullvideo {
66          display: none;
67      }
68  }
69
```

When resizing it though, it will show white space. We fix that by setting negative margins, which makes the viewport much wider, and allows us to center the content on screen:

```
51  @media (min-aspect-ratio: 16/9) {
52      .fullvideo {
53          height: 300%;
54          top: -100%;
55          width: 300%;
56          left: -100%;
57      }
58  }
```

A key point to note is the values used for height, top, left, and width; although these seem extreme, they are required to help center the video on screen when viewing the content with a 16/9 aspect ratio set.

Perfect! Our video plays well. We can see the content without too much difficulty. Everything should be good, surely? Well, yes and no; concepts such as background video are not without their risks; it's important to understand where things might fall over if we're not careful. Let's pause for a moment and consider some of the potential traps that might upset the proverbial apple cart, if we're not careful with our video.

Exploring the risks

In our previous example, we explored the concept of adding video as background content. It's a fashion that has taken off within the last couple of years, and provides an interesting effect, that is different to seeing the standard images we might otherwise see!

It's not without a certain element of risk though; there are a few pointers we must consider, when adding video as the background content:

- It's possible to add video, but we shouldn't just add it because we can—any video we add using this method must amplify the site's overall message.
- Any video added will likely be set to autoplay, but the sound must be muted by default—if possible, it shouldn't have any sound at all.
- Does our video fit with the site brand, tone, color palette, and so on? There is no point building a killer site, only to ruin it with a rubbish video.
- Costs are something we must consider; it can be expensive to host video content, so it must be compressed as much as possible to keep file sizes down, and in a suitable format that works on multiple devices, including mobile.
- Our video should not be too long; we must strike a balance between making it too long and not long enough so that it does not feel too repetitive.
- Accessibility is a key pointer; it must be of sufficiently high contrast so as to make the text overlay legible.
- Our video may look good, but what about performance? Your customers will not thank you if you produce a lightning fast site, but slow it down with a large, poorly optimized video as a background; they will very likely vote with their feet!
- The compatibility technique we've used doesn't work on IE8, so a static placeholder must be included as a fallback; in the event the browser we use doesn't support HTML5 video or its attributes (such as autoplay, for mobiles).

Even though we have some clear pointers that should be considered, it should not stop us from using this effect; I'm one for pushing out the boundaries of what is possible, provided we do it well!

Making audio responsive

Question—we've worked on making videos responsive, but what about audio content?

Well, we can apply similar principles to the HTML5 `<audio>` element; instead of setting a specific width, we can use max-width and set a percentage figure to control how wide it displays on the screen.

The code to achieve this is very simple, and should by now be familiar—let's take a look at what is involved:

1. For this demo, we need to avail ourselves of suitable files; for licensing reasons, you won't find any in the code download that accompanies this book, unfortunately! One way to achieve this is to take a copy of an iTunes file (normally in `.m4a` format), then use an online service such as Media.io (`http://media.io/`) to convert it to the right formats. You will need to convert to both MP3 and OGG formats, before continuing with this demo.

2. Assuming we now have the right files, go ahead and extract a copy of `audioelement.html` from the code download that accompanies this book, and save it to the root of our project area.

3. Next, at the root of our project area, go ahead and create a new folder called `audio`; into it, save copies of the audio files you either have or created from step 1.

4. In a new file go ahead and add the following code, saving it as `audioelement.css` in the `css` subfolder at the root of our project area:

```
audio {
    max-width: 100%;
    width: 800px;
}
```

5. Try previewing the results of our work in a browser—if all is well, we should see something akin to this screenshot:

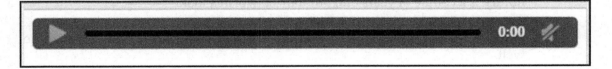

At first glance, it may not look special, but then the `<audio>` element isn't meant to look anything out of the ordinary! The key here though is when we resize the browser window; we've set a max width value of `100%`, but have constrained this by setting an upper limit of `50rem` in the width attribute. No matter how many times we resize our window, the audio player will fill the full width, but not go any wider than `50rem`.

 Unlike the `<video>` element, we can't resize the height using just CSS; to do this requires overriding the `<audio>` element with jQuery, which is out of the scope of this book.

Let's move on and put our new-found knowledge to the test to create a practical example—how about making a video fullscreen, and responding to changes in the browser viewport automatically? Setting up video using this technique is always fraught with controversy, but I'm not one to shy away from a challenge, so without further ado, let's dive in and see why we must step carefully when using video at fullscreen.

Taking things further

Throughout the course of this book, we've concentrated on using the core technologies of HTML5 and CSS3; in many cases, this is all we need, but there will come a time when we have to use other technologies to help fulfill a task, as we've outgrown the art of possible with plain CSS and HTML code.

Thankfully, there are lots of options available online to help with making videos responsive, and to take our skills. It goes without saying though that we should always ask ourselves if our need for another library is because the realities of life mean that we can't achieve our task without using it or if we've simply become too lazy!

If indeed we do need to download and use an additional library, there are a few good options to try out, which include:

- **FluidVids**: It is available from `http://toddmotto.com/labs/fluidvids`; the library is a couple of years old, but may be worth a look.
- **responsiveVideo**: It is downloadable from `http://cbavota.bitbucket.org/res ponsive-video/`. This has been around for a couple of years, so may not work so well.
- **Embed Responsively**: It is hosted at `http://embedresponsively.com/`, and will return appropriate embed code for any of the major video hosting companies, such as YouTube; it's also responsive to boot!

- **FitVids.js**: This plugin, available from `http://fitvidsjs.com` and built by Chris Coyier of CSS Tricks' fame, may be worth a look, although it hasn't been updated for at least 2-3 years.
- **MediaElement.js**: It is available from `http://mediaelementjs.com`, and is a great library that works with both the `<video>` and `<audio>` elements; it allows us to override the standard element and customize it to our requirements using jQuery and CSS. There are plenty of examples of doing this online, along with suitable tutorials on how to achieve a custom look and feel to any player we skin using jQuery.

A small word of caution—a number of the video plugin libraries for jQuery haven't been updated for some time; you may well find that they no longer work properly with more recent versions of jQuery. This isn't necessarily a bad thing, as support for the HTML5 `<video>` and `<audio>` elements is now excellent; this renders many of these libraries surplus to requirements!

 Some of you may ask why we need to use jQuery to skin either HTML5 audio or video players; many of the individual elements are not accessible using plain CSS, and need JavaScript to expose those elements before styling them with CSS.

Phew! We're almost through this part of the journey, but before we move onto taking a look at using media queries in the next chapter, there is one more part of making responsive content; how about the text we have on our sites? It might not immediately strike you as being one we would associate with videos and text (at least in the context of making content responsive), but all will shortly become clear.

Making text fit on screen

When building sites, it goes without saying but our designs clearly must start somewhere—this is usually with adding text. It's therefore essential that we allow for this in our responsive designs at the same time.

Now is a perfect opportunity to explore how to make our text fluid and fill the available space. Although text is not media in the same way as images or video, it is still content that has to be added at some point to our pages! With this in mind, let's dive in and explore how we can make our text responsive.

Sizing with em units

When working on non-responsive sites, it's likely that sizes will be quoted in pixel values; it's a perfectly acceptable way of working. However, if we begin to make our sites responsive, then content won't resize well using pixel values; we have to use something else.

There are two alternatives: em or rem units. The former is based on setting a base font size that in most browsers defaults to 16px; in this example, the equivalent pixel sizes are given in the comments that follow each rule:

```
h1 { font-size: 2.4em; }    /* 38px */
p  { line-height: 1.4em; }  /* 22px */
```

Unfortunately, there is an inherent problem with using em units; if we nest elements, then font sizes will be compounded, as em units are calculated relative to its parent. For example, if the font size of a list element is set at 1.4em (22px), then the font size of a list item within a list becomes 30.8em (1.4 x 22px).

To work around these issues, we can use rem values as a replacement, these are calculated from the root element, in place of the parent element. If you look carefully throughout many of the demos created for this book, you will see rem units being used to define the sizes of elements in the demos.

Using rem units as a replacement

The rem (or root em) unit is set to be relative to the root, instead of the parent; it means that we eliminate any issues with compounding at a stroke, as our reference point remains constant, and is not affected by other elements on the page.

The downside of this is support—rem units are not supported in IE7 or 8, so if we still have to support these browsers, then we must fall back to using pixel or em values instead. This of course raises the question: should we still support these browsers, or is their usage of our site so small as to not be worth the effort required to update our code?

If the answer is that we must support IE8 or below, then we can take a hybrid approach; we can set both pixel/em and rem values at the same time in our code:

```
.article-body {
  font-size: 1.125rem;  /* 18 / 16 */
  font-size: 18px;
}

.caps, figure, footer {
  font-size: 0.875rem;  /* 14 / 16 */
  font-size: 14px;
}
```

Notice how we set rem values first? Browsers that support rem units will use these first; the ones that don't can automatically fall back to using pixel or em values instead. The values in each comment are the pixel equivalents; if, for example, we divide 18px by 16px (as the base value for all sizes), we would arrive at 1.125, as indicated in the text.

Exploring use of viewport units

If we want to take it further, then there is another alternative we can explore; how about using viewport units?

These effectively combine the best of both worlds; a viewport unit (or 1vw) is 1% of the viewport axis. So, if we had a viewport of 50 cm wide, a single vw unit would be 0.5 cm. We can specify sizes in the same way as we would do for pixel, em, or rem units. Take a look at this little extract, which gives a flavor of what it would look like:

```
h1 { font-size: 5.9vw; }
h2 { font-size: 3.0vh; }
p { font-size: 2vmin; }
```

The beauty though is no matter what size the viewport, the font size will always appear correctly, as it will automatically resize if the view port is changed.

 To see a simple example of this in action, browse to http://codepen.io/a libby251/pen/xOGrqN and try resizing the browser window. See how the text automatically changes size, with no loss of quality?

Taking things further

Okay, at this point, we've added responsive capabilities to our text; our sites are looking pretty good….I can see a *but* coming….

At present, support for responsive text (and in particular vw or rem units) is excellent; browsers that will choke on these two units are few and far between. However, there *may* come a time when we need additional help; unlike images or video content, there are not many options available to choose from! The two best examples are FlowType.js, available from `http://simplefocus.com/flowtype/`, and FitText.js, from `http://fittextjs.com/`.

The catch though is that these libraries haven't been updated for 2-3 years, so are not likely to work with recent versions of jQuery. It's a good indicator of how well responsive text has come along over the years, and that we really should be using it natively, rather than relying on JavaScript!

Summary

A key part of any website must be the media used; after all, it would become boring without some form of color! This is no different for responsive sites; throughout the course of this chapter, we've covered some useful techniques for adding responsive media, so let's reflect on what we've covered in this chapter.

We kicked off with a look at making images fluid, which is the basic concept behind responsive media; we then swiftly moved on to look at using the HTML5 `<picture>` element, to see how it can be used to specify different sized images based on hardware capabilities. We explored a few pointers on what is available to use, should we decide to that existing native support is insufficient, and we need to progress from using just plain HTML and CSS.

Next up came a look at responsive video; we examined how to make externally hosted videos responsive, with just plain CSS. We also covered the techniques required to make the HTML5 `<video>` element responsive, if hosting externally is not an option. We also explored the HTML5 `<audio>` element, and saw how we can use similar techniques to make it responsive.

We then rounded off the chapter with a look at making standard text responsive; we covered how this has already been used in many demos throughout the book, before exploring the different techniques, such as using em or rem values, which are often better than standard pixel units. We then finished with a quick demo on using viewport units for font sizes, so we could see how to get the best of everything when creating responsive text.

Phew—a lot covered! Let's move on. Now that we have our layout and content in place, we need to consider how to resize them correctly. Enter media queries—this will be the subject of our next chapter.

4
Exploring Media Queries

Mobile to overtake fixed Internet access by 2014.

This bold prediction from Mary Meeker, an analyst from KPCB, back in 2008 came true in 2013-14, when mobile Internet usage rose to 51% in the USA, overtaking desktop for the first time. Part of this can be attributed to the use of media queries, the basic principles of which haven't changed since their official introduction in 2000.

Today, queries exist to support anything from high-resolution images to monochrome screens and handheld devices; throughout the course of this chapter, we'll continue with the theme of discovering what is possible with just a browser and text editor, and show you that it isn't always necessary to download anything to create media queries when building responsive sites.

In this chapter, we will cover the following topics:

- Understanding the basics of media queries
- Creating breakpoints and removing the need for them
- Exploring best practice and common mistakes
- Taking things further

Curious? Let's get cracking.

Exploring some examples

Open a browser; let's go and visit some sites.

Now, you may think I've lost my marbles, but stay with me. I want to show you a few examples. Let's take a look at a couple of example sites at different screen widths. How about this example from my favorite coffee company, Starbucks:

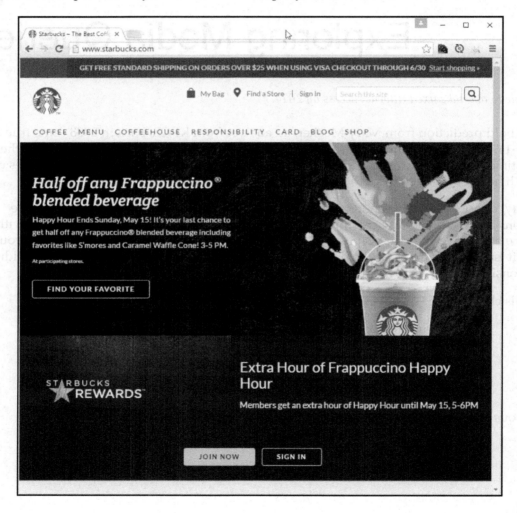

Try resizing the browser window; if you get small enough, you will see something akin to this:

Here's another example—we cannot forget the site for the publisher of this book, Packt:

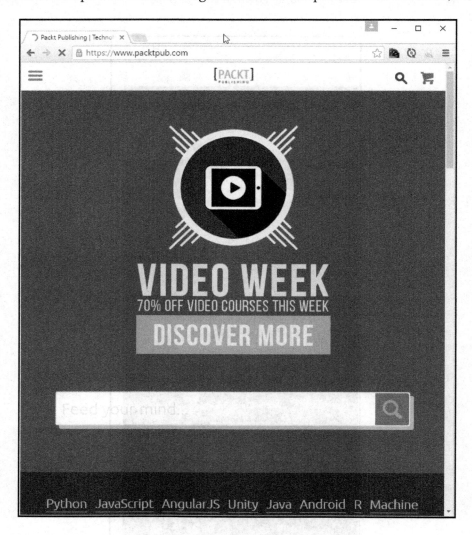

Try changing the size of your browser window. If we resize it enough, it will show this:

For our third and final example, let's go visit CSS Tricks, the site created by Chris Coyier, at `http://www.css-tricks.com`:

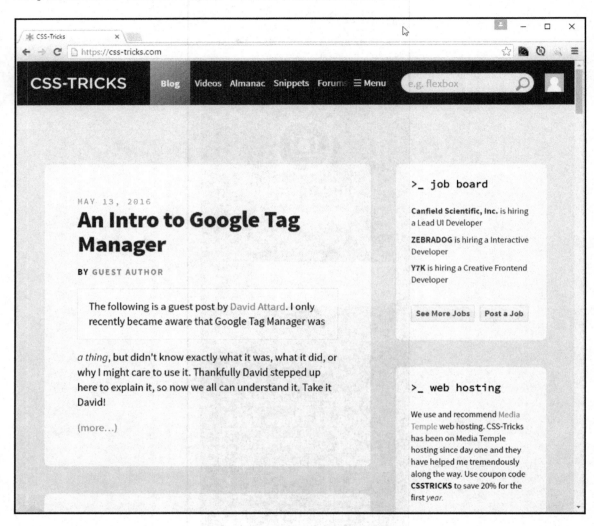

If we resize this to a smaller width, this is what we will get:

Now, what was the point of all that, I hear you ask? Well, it's simple. All of them use media queries in some form or other; CSS Tricks uses the queries built into WordPress, Packt's site is hosted using Drupal, and Starbucks' site is based around the Handlebars template system.

The key here is that all use media queries to determine what should be displayed; throughout the course of this chapter, we'll explore using them in more detail, and see how we can use them to better manage content in responsive sites. Let's make a start with exploring their make up in more detail.

Understanding media queries

The developer Bruce Lee sums it up perfectly, when likening the effects of media queries to how water acts in different containers:

Empty your mind, be formless, shapeless—like water. Now you put water in a cup, it becomes the cup; you put water into a bottle it becomes the bottle; you put it in a teapot it becomes the teapot. Now water can flow or it can crash. Be water, my friend.

We can use media queries to apply different CSS styles, based on available screen estate or specific device characteristics. These might include, but not be limited to the type of display, screen resolution, or display density. Media queries work on the basis of testing to see if certain conditions are true, using this format:

```
@media [not|only] [mediatype] and ([media feature]) {
    // CSS code;
}
```

We can use a similar principle to determine if entire style sheets should be loaded, instead of individual queries:

```
<link rel="stylesheet" media="mediatype and|only|not (media feature)"
href="myStyle.css">
```

Seems pretty simple, right? The great thing about media queries is that we don't need to download or install any additional software to use or create them; we can build most of them in the browser directly.

Exploring the available media types

If we take a look at the example query in the previous section, we see that part of it is made up of the type of media in use. This is just part of the query. All media queries come in two parts, with the first part controlling how our CSS will be displayed, with the second part taking care of when it is displayed.

Take a look at this example:

```
<!-- CSS media query on a link element -->
<link rel="stylesheet" media="(max-width: 800px)" href="example.css" />

<!-- CSS media query within a stylesheet -->
<style>
@media (max-width: 757px) {
  .sidebar {
    display: none;
  }
}
</style>
```

This illustrates two ways of referencing media queries: the first example doesn't specify the media type, so we can infer it will be all by default; the second part of it states that it will only apply when the width of our window is at least 800px.

The second media query one doesn't specify the media type either, so again all will be inferred as the default; this time, the .sidebar element will not be displayed if the window width is less than 600px wide.

Let's see what all media types can be used:

Value	Used for
all	All types of media
print	Printers or printing content to media
screen	Screens/displays (such as computers, mobiles, or tablets)
speech	Screen readers
braille	Braille tactile feedback devices
embossed	Paged braille printers
handheld	Handheld devices, except smartphones and tablets, which use screen instead
print	Paged material and for documents viewed on screen in print preview mode
projection	Projecting presentations
screen	Color computer screens and smartphones
speech	Speech synthesizers
tty	Media using a fixed-pitch character grid (such as teletypes, terminals, or portable devices with limited display capabilities

In addition, to this, we have a number of features that we can use to control the trigger for displaying the content; it's worth getting to know them, as they all play an important role, but work in different ways. Let's take a look at the list in more detail and learn what each of them does in turn.

Listing the available media features

Adding a query that specifies the media target is only half the picture; we also need to give it something that controls when to display it! To achieve this, we can provide one or more conditions that must be satisfied in order for content to be styled or displayed.

Let's have a look at some of the options available:

Name of the attribute	Description
aspect-ratio	Viewport's width:height ratio
device-aspect-ratio	Device's width:height ratio
device-[height|width]	Height or width of device's screen
height	Viewport's height
min-device-pixel-ratio	Check device's pixel ratio. Good for high definition and retina devices (where the ratio is greater than 2)
[min|max]-aspect-ratio	Viewport's minimum or maximum width:height ratio
[min|max]-device-aspect-ratio	Device's minimum or maximum width:height ratio
[min|max]-device-height	Device's minimum or maximum height or width
[min|max]-width	Viewport's minimum or maximum width
orientation	Viewport's orientation in portrait or landscape mode
resolution	Device's resolution (in dpi or dpcm)
width	Viewport's width

The key here is selecting the right attribute against which we should run our test; a great example is checking orientation so that we can determine if a tablet is in portrait or landscape mode. We will make good use of some of these query tests later in this chapter.

Okay, time to move on. The theme so far has been what we can achieve by just using a browser and a text editor. This may seem limiting at first, but I maintain that too many people resort to using additional help (such as using jQuery) to create queries when it isn't always necessary to do so. In the main this will work, but there are some points that we should consider:

- Do you need to support IE8 or below? If so, then we need to provide additional support for this; a decision by Microsoft in early 2016 though means that IE8 is no longer supported, so now is the time to really consider if this browser should feature in your designs.

- Support for some of the newer media queries, such as max resolution, is only available in the newer browsers; it's worth checking the CanIUse.com site and your server logs to confirm if not supporting older browsers will be an issue.
- If we need to provide fallback support, then don't automatically assume this means we must use a JavaScript-based solution; it's worth considering what support you need to offer, and whether you really need to use media queries (more on this anon).

Okay, let's move on: it's time to get physical, and stuck into something more practical! We've covered some of the different facets that make up queries and explored some of the considerations we need to allow for, when working with just a browser and text editor. Before we get too practical though, we need to cover one more topic. There are occasions when we need to test for multiple conditions. We can do this using logical operators. Let's take a quick look at some of these in more detail.

Introducing operators in our queries

When composing media queries that require multiple tests, we can make use of logical operators to confirm if one or more CSS rules should be applied to our content. If we use logical operators, we need to encapsulate each attribute that is tested in parentheses; otherwise, it will generate an error in our code.

Let's take a look at some of the more common examples of operators:

- **And**: It is used to combine multiple media types or media features into a single complex query. It works normally like arithmetic and operators, that is, requires each condition to be true to execute the query.
- **Not**: We can use this to negate a query. It applies on the whole media query and works only if the entire query would otherwise return false (such as `min-width: 700px` on a `600px` display). This operator must be used with a media type.
- **Only**: It is used to apply styles only when we need to prevent applying selected styles in old browsers.

> Media queries are case sensitive, and will return false if unknown media types are encountered.

So far, we've talked about the basics of what a media query looks like: let's explore how we can use them to manage content by identifying where our designs break at different screen sizes. These breaks, or **breakpoints**, are what make media queries work – whilst it is clearly key that we get them right, it is also important to know when we should and should not use them…

Identifying common breakpoints

In an age of responsive design, breakpoints are key to a successful site; it's all about defining where our design might break, if we were to resize the available screen width. It is important to understand that no two sites will have identical queries in use; this said, there are some we can use that can be used as a basis for our designs.

We'll start with this one, for standard desktops:

```
@media only screen and (max-width: 768px){
   /* CSS Styles */
}
```

With the meteoric rise in mobiles, we can't forget those who are fortunate enough to own a smartphone, such as an iPhone:

```
@media only screen and (min-device-width: 320px) and (max-device-width:
480px) {
   /* Styles */
}
```

The downside of this query means that it would equally apply to any device that was small enough to satisfy the `*-device-width` dimensions given. This is not what we want (or intended); to set a cleaner division between mobile devices and desktops, we can adapt the query thus:

```
@media only screen and (max-device-width: 320px) {
   /* Styles - for mobiles in portrait mode */
}
```

This one is for mobiles in landscape mode:

```
@media only screen and (min-device-width: 321px) {
  /* Styles - for mobiles in landscape mode */
}
```

Taking it even further, we can also cater for tablets, such as iPads:

```
@media only screen and (min-device-width: 768px) and (max-device-width:
1024px) {
  /* Styles */
}
```

A similar caveat applies here though – we've not set a sufficiently clear threshold that can only apply to tablets. We can fix that, by adding the `orientation` attribute:

```
@media only screen and (min-device-width: 768px) and (max-device-width :
1024px) and (orientation : portrait) {
  /* Styles */
}
```

To complete the picture, we can equally apply a check for when tablet content is being displayed in landscape mode:

```
@media only screen and (min-device-width: 768px) and (max-device-width :
1024px) and (orientation : landscape) {
  /* Styles */
}
```

These breakpoints are just a small selection of what could be used to add media queries to any site; this does not mean we should use them blindly; we should only add those queries that allow us to support our target devices. We can of course add custom queries, although there is a risk that we can add more than is necessary. Let's take a moment to consider the implications of adding custom queries, and why this can become an issue for our projects.

 It's worth researching what others have created as media queries online; there are dozens of examples available, some of which will be geared toward specific devices, such as smartphones or tablets.

Creating custom breakpoints

The media queries we've already outlined should cover a wide range of scenarios; there will be occasions when these won't suffice, and our site isn't working as expected.

What do we do? Well, we are not limited to using the standard queries we've already covered; we can absolutely create our own!

Creating a custom breakpoint is very easy, as long as we do it the right way; done incorrectly, and we can create unnecessary breaks that have a limited use or an unintended knock-on effect to other devices. To see what we mean, let's work through a (theoretical) example.

Imagine your site has been resized to around 335px, and we see it is a little out of kilter—there are a number of elements that don't quite fit properly. To better manage content at this breakpoint, the temptation would be to write a query such as this:

```
@media only screen and (max-device-width: 345px){
  /* Styles */
}
```

We would add our changes in the area headed by /*Styles*/.

Sounds reasonable, right? It would be, if it weren't for one thing: we've now just created a whole new set of problems for viewing devices that have a width lower than 345px!

The key to solving this issue is to not simply use a bigger pixel value, as this may break the layout for other devices—this includes mobile devices, in portrait or landscape modes. The right way to fix this is to identify the exact circumstances where our query fails, and to either adjust the query to better match the circumstances or (ideally) work out if the design itself can be tweaked to avoid the need for a query.

So, for example, if our site broke between 325px and 345px, and that the failure was in portrait mode only, we would create a media query such as this one:

```
@media only screen and (min-device-width : 325px) and (max-device-width :
345px) and (orientation : portrait) {
  /* Styles */
}
```

How does this help us? Well, refining our query to be more explicit avoids any possible conflict with more generic queries that we might have already created. We're also making the threshold limits clearer too; we won't trigger the query unless we can match all three conditions at the same time.

Understanding the rationale

Some developers may ask why we simply don't just fix the available viewport; this changes size when we change orientation, so surely the content will adjust to fit, right?

Well, yes and no. It's all about understanding where content is positioned, and the types of devices we want to support, in addition to desktops. We should not forget that it is perfectly valid to have a layout that is different in portrait mode to those in landscape; try looking at Packt's site in landscape and portrait modes on an iPad!

At the time of writing, an extra element is displayed in portrait mode, but it is not present in landscape orientation. If one of the elements in the portrait mode was broken and not displaying correctly, then simply specifying numerical breakpoints will not work. To fix the issue, we must also specify the affected orientation, otherwise fixing one mode may break another.

Taking care over our design

Okay, so we've created a bunch of media queries, ready for implementing into a site. We're good to move on and start building some examples, or are we? If I said to hold fire for a moment, you would very likely think I've lost my marbles; but as always, there is a good reason. Let me explain.

A drawback when using media queries is that no two sites will be the same; this means that we can't always reuse standard queries in multiple sites. There will be times when we have to create custom breakpoints to satisfy a requirement for a site; the trick is to know when and where our site may need extra attention, over and above the normal breakpoints we might have used in our site.

Creating custom, ad hoc queries is easy, but we do run the risk of creating too many, which undermines the whole concept of responsive design. Can we get around this? Well, yes we can; it involves a shift in our approach to designing, which is not to focus on viewport sizes, but our content instead.

Removing the need for breakpoints

Up until now, we've covered how we can use breakpoints to control what is displayed, and when, according to which device is being used. Let's assume you're working on a project for a client and have created a series of queries that use values such as 320px, 480px, 768px, and 1024px to cover support for a good range of devices.

No matter what our design looks like, we will always be faced with two issues if we focus on using specific screen viewports as the basis for controlling our designs:

- Keeping up with the sheer number of devices that are available
- The inflexibility of limiting our screen width

So, hold on. We've created breakpoints, yet this can end up causing us more problems? If we're finding ourselves creating lots of media queries that address specific problems (in addition to standard ones), then we will start to lose the benefits of a responsive site; instead we should re-examine our site to understand why the design isn't working and see if we can't tweak it so as to remove the need for the custom query.

Ultimately, our site and target devices will dictate what is required—a good rule of thumb is if we are creating more custom queries than a standard bunch of four to six breakpoints, then perhaps it is time to recheck our design!

As an alternative to working with specific screen sizes, there is a different approach we can take, which is to follow the principle of adaptive design and not responsive design. Instead of simply specifying a number of fixed screen sizes (such as for the iPhone 6 Plus or a Samsung Galaxy unit), we build our designs around the point at which the *design begins to fail*.

Why? The answer is simple. The idea here is to come up with different bands, where designs will work between a lower and upper value, instead of simply specifying a query that checks for fixed screen sizes that are lower or above certain values. Don't worry for now if it doesn't entirely make sense just yet; for now, the key here is that we're creating designs that mean we can reduce the need to support so many devices.

Let's put this theory into practice, and start creating some demos to show off how we can use media queries in practice.

Putting our theory into practice

Throughout the course of this chapter, we've covered the different parts that make up media queries as I am sure someone once said, *it is time*.

Yes, it's time to put this into practice. Before we start creating some real-world examples, let's create something we can use to explore the effects of adding a media query to code. We'll start by resizing some simple boxes on screen:

1. From the code download, go ahead and extract a copy of `queryexample.html` and save it to our project area.

2. In a text editor, go ahead and add the following styles; we'll start with some basic styles for our boxes:

```
body { background-color: #F3ECDD; text-align: center;
    font-family: Arial, sans-serif; color: #ffffff;
    min-width: 33%; }

.box { width: 100%; background: #905f20; border-radius: 0.625em;
    margin: 0; }

.box2{ min-width: 100%; background: #6b8e6f; border-radius:
    0.625rem;
    float: left; }

h3:after{ content: ' is less than 30rem'; }
```

3. We then need to add our media query; go ahead and add this below the closing bracket of the previous style rule:

```
@media screen and (min-width: 30rem) {
    body { background-color: #C7B47C; }

    .box { width: 49.5%; float: left; }

    .box + .box { margin-left: 1%; margin-bottom: 0.625em; }

    h3:after{ content: ' is greater than 30rem'; }
}
```

4. Save the file as `queryexample.css` within the `css` subfolder in our project area.

If we try previewing the results of our work by running `queryexample.css`, we should see something akin to this screenshot:

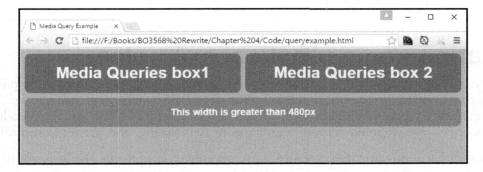

Let's understand what happened here. In the core CSS (in step 3), we added three `<div>` elements to our markup. Since we gave them `100%` width and height is set to `auto` by default, they'll be stacked as a series of boxes.

If we use Chrome and activate the device mode as we did before, then we can begin to see the effect of resizing the browser window. If we resize it to below `30rem` in width as our breakpoint (or `480px`), we can see the boxes realign and resize at the same time; the background also changes to a light brown color:

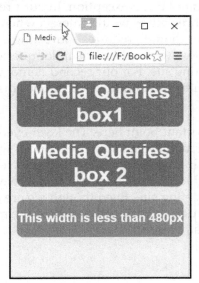

Now that we've seen the basics of setting up queries, let's take this a step further and create some practical examples. We'll begin with setting up a simple web page to which we will apply some simple media queries.

Creating some practical examples

Over the next few pages, we'll be exploring how we can make good use of media queries; we'll be constructing two demos that illustrate some of the ways we can use queries. The demos themselves may not look complicated, but this is not a bad thing; making code complex only serves to make it more fragile, prone to breaking, and harder to support.

Let's take a look at our first demo, which adds responsive support to a basic portfolio template page.

Making it real

Making it real—what a title! There is a good reason for it. When exploring new concepts, one of my pet hates is exploring a demo that is so minimalistic as to not include anything that gives a true picture of the functionality that I want to begin using in my development.

Creating media queries should not be an exception. In our previous example, we created some test queries to see how three boxes would interact when the browser window is resized. To put this into context though, requires something a little more in-depth; one could do worse than explore how we might add similar queries to a portfolio page that might be part of a new or existing site. For our second demo, we're going to create a simple web page template, then begin to add and develop queries that allow it to be used on mobile devices.

 There is an important point here. The keen-eyed among you will notice that this is not a mobile-first approach, which we advocated earlier in the book. Yes, mobile-first is absolutely the preferred approach, but we live in a world where this may not be possible, and we may have to add query support to an existing site. Even though we are doing this in what is not our preferred order, the principles around the media queries used in the next demo will still apply.

Let's make a start:

1. To start, we need to extract a number of files from the code download that accompanies this book; go ahead and save copies of `responsive.html`, the two `coffeebeans.png` images (normal and small size) and the `video` folder, to the root of our project area. Move the two images into the `img` folder within this folder.

2. In a new file, add the following styles and save it as `responsive.css` within the `css` folder of our project area. The first block of styles create the main text area and overall container for our demo:

```
#wrapper { width: 96%; max-width: 45rem; margin: auto; padding: 2%;
   border: 1px solid #000; margin-top: 3rem; border-radius: 0.2rem;
   margin-bottom: 3rem; }
#wrapper > header > img { display: none; }

#main { width: 60%; margin-right: 5%; float: left; }
```

3. This deals with the `Skip to...` at the top of the mobile view; it's hidden for now, but will be visible when the media query is activated:

```
#skipTo { display: none; }
#skipTo li { background: #197a8a; }
#skipTo a { color: #fff; font-size: 0.8rem; }
```

4. We need something to host our video and banner image; these styles take care of that for us:

```
#video-wrapper { padding-bottom: 2rem; }
#video-wrapper video  { max-width: 100%; }

#banner { float: left; margin-bottom: 0.9375rem; width: 100%; }
#banner { height: 15rem; width: 44.5rem; background-image:
   url('../img/coffeebeans.png'); max-width: 100%; }
```

5. We have a side area on the right of our main demo window; we need a style to control its dimensions:

```
aside { width: 35%; float: right; }
```

6. A number of links are used in our site, mainly in the form of buttons. This takes care of their styling:

```
a { text-decoration: none; text-transform: uppercase; }
a, img { border: medium none; color: #000; font-weight: bold;
  outline: medium none; }
```

7. A key part of the site is of course the navigation. These style rules manage the presentation, which is based around a number of unordered list items:

```
header { font-family: 'Droid Sans', sans-serif; }
header h1 { height: 70px; float: left; display: block;
  font-weight: 700; font-size: 2rem; }
header nav { float: right; margin-top: 2.5rem; height: 1.375rem;
  border-radius: 0.25rem; }
header nav li { display: inline; margin-left: 0.9375rem; }
header nav ul { font-weight: 400; font-size: 1.1rem; }
header nav a { padding: 0.3125rem 0.3125rem 0.3125rem 0.3125rem; }
header nav a:hover { background-color: #8e5f57; color: #fff;
  border-radius: 0.25rem; }
```

8. Last but by no means least, we need something to make our footer presentable:

```
footer { border-top: 0.0625rem solid #ccc; clear: both;
  height: 1.875rem; padding-top: 0.3125rem; }
```

9. Save the file. We now need to add our media queries. Leave two lines in our style sheet, then add the following code:

```
@media screen and (max-width: 414px) and (orientation: portrait) {
  #header { background-color: #8e5f57; }
  #wrapper { min-width: 15.63rem; border: none; margin-top: 0; }
  #wrapper > header > img { float: right; display: block; }

  #skipTo { display: none; }
  #skipTo a { padding: 0.625rem; text-align: center;
    height: 1.25rem; background-color: #8e5f57; }
  #main {float: left; clear: left; margin: 0 0 0.625rem;
    width: 100%; margin-top: 10rem; }

  #banner { display: none; }
  aside {float: left; clear: left;margin: 0 0 0.625rem;
    width: 100%; }

  header h1 {margin-top: 1.25rem; height: 2.1875rem; }
  header nav {float: left; clear: left; margin: 0 0 0.625rem;
    width: 100%; border-radius: none; }
```

```
      header nav li  {margin: 0; background: #efefef; display: block;
         margin-bottom: 0.1875rem; height: 2.5rem; }
      header nav a  {display: block;  padding: 0.625rem;
         text-align: center; }
      header nav a:hover { border-radius: none; }
   }
```

10. Leave another two blank lines below the first media query, then add the following code:

```
@media screen and (max-width: 736px) and (orientation: landscape) {
   #header { background-color: #8e5f57; }

   #wrapper { min-width: 15.63rem; border: none; margin-top: 0; }
   #wrapper > header > img { float: right; display: block; }

   #skipTo { display: none; }
   #skipTo a { padding: 0.625rem; text-align: center;
      height: 1.25rem; background-color: #8e5f57; }
   #main {float: left; clear: left; margin: 0 0 0.625rem;
      width: 100%; margin-top: 10rem; }

   #banner { display: none; }
   aside {float: left; clear: left;margin: 0 0 0.625rem;
      width: 100%; }

   header h1 {margin-top: 1.25rem; height: 2.188rem; }
   header nav  {float: left; clear: left; margin: 0 0 0.625rem;
      width: 100%; border-radius: none; }
   header nav li { margin: 0; background: #efefef; display: block;
      margin-bottom: 0.1875rem; height: 2.5rem; }
   header nav a  { display: block;  padding: 0.625rem;
      text-align: center; }
   header nav a:hover { border-radius: none; }
}
```

11. Save the file, then preview the results in a browser. Ideally, this should be Google Chrome or an alternative such as Firefox:

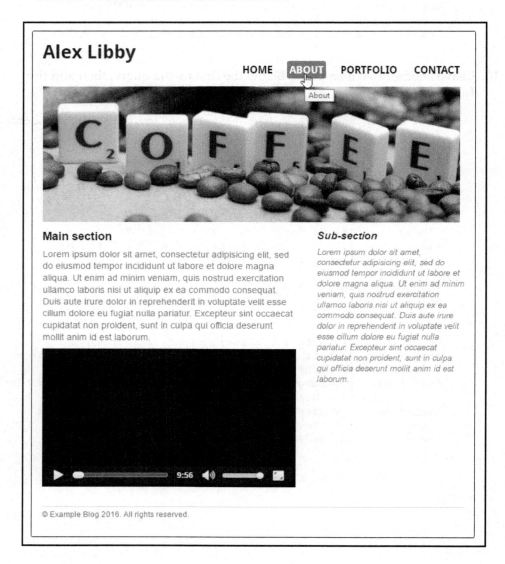

A perfectly presentable page, I hope you will agree. It shows off two of my favorite things perfectly: my love of coffee and the Scrabble board game! I always say coffee must be the secret tool in many developers' armories, but I digress…

Try resizing the screen; for argument's sake, let's resize it to **414 x 736**, or the equivalent required for an **iPhone 6 Plus**:

We can use Chrome's device mode to switch the orientation to landscape:

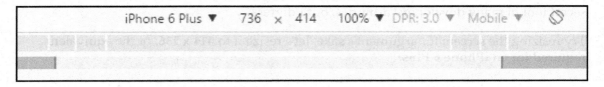

We can see that the site realigns itself:

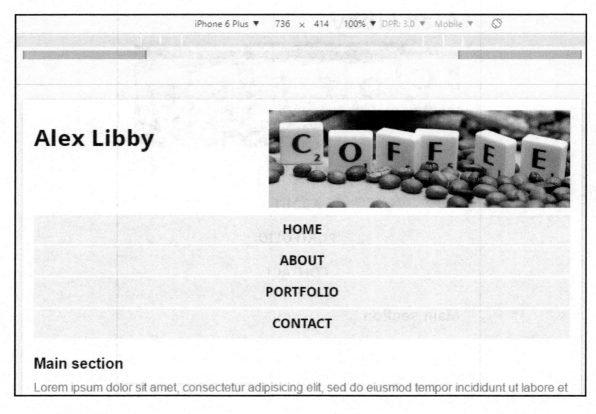

It's a simple, clean design. The key here is that we can use this as a basis for adding more queries that support other devices. There are some important concepts that we should explore in more detail, so let's take five for a moment, and see how media queries play their part in our demo.

Exploring what happened

Many of the styles used in this example cater for styling our page; the key rules for us start on lines 33 and 50, where we style for an iPhone 6 Plus in portrait and landscape modes, respectively. Let's take a look at these two rules in more detail:

```
@media screen and (max-width: 414px) and (orientation: portrait) {
...
}
```

This rule states that the screen width must have a max-width of 414px or less; if it is bigger and still showing in portrait mode, then the rule will not apply.

Within this rule, we've taken styles already used in the main block and applied changes that allow us to maintain the desired effect when viewing the site on an iPhone. A perfect example is the #banner block; in the main set of styles, we set a number of attributes to position it on screen:

```
#banner { float: left; margin-bottom: 0.9375rem; width: 100%; }
#banner { height: 15rem; width: 44.5rem; background-image:
url('../img/coffeebeans.png');  max-width: 100%; }
```

However, that won't suit being displayed on an iPhone, leaving aside how big the image is at 717px by 214px. It also weighs in at a hefty 102KB! Clearly, we don't want to keep downloading such a large image on a mobile device (where Internet access is likely to be metered), so we need to do something else.

Instead, we have a smaller version in use, in the form of coffeebeans-small.png. This one is a more palatable 33KB, and sits in the top-right corner of our page when viewed on a mobile in portrait mode. We hide the original as it is not needed:

```
@media screen and (max-width: 414px) and (orientation: portrait) {
...
  #wrapper > header > img { float: right; display: block; }
...
  #banner { display: none; }
}
```

As soon as we flip to using it in landscape mode, this rule kicks in:

```
@media screen and (max-width: 736px) and (orientation: landscape) {
...
  #wrapper > header > img { float: right; display: block; }
...
  #banner { display: none; }
}
```

Notice though we don't need to change the rule. The image stays the same size and is already set to float to the right, so the rule can simply be reused. We have to specify it here too; otherwise, it won't display at all. To see the difference, try setting the demo using Google Chrome to emulate iPad mode:

```
▼ <header>
  ▶ <nav id="skipTo">…</nav>          #banner {                          responsive.css:14
    <h1>Alex Libby</h1>                 height: 15rem;
    <img src="img/coffeebeans-          width: 44.5rem;
    small.png">                         background-image: url('../img/coffeebeans.png');
  ▶ <nav>…</nav>                        max-width: 100%;
    <div id="banner"></div>  == $0   }
  </header>                           #banner {                          responsive.css:13
  ▶ <section id="main">…</section>      float: left;
```

We can see that even though the base code uses `coffeebeans-small.png` in the `#banner` `<div>`, our media queries have replaced it with `coffeebeans.png`.

 You may notice that the media query widths are not set in rem units; this is purely so we can match them with the Device tool in Chrome. You can easily set them to rem units if you prefer to do so.

We've purposely kept the rules in our demo simple; they illustrate how, with little effort, we can get our page to display properly in both desktop, iPhone 6 portrait and iPhone 6 landscape modes perfectly. We can then reuse the same principles to extend support to cover other devices; the trick is to make sure that we use a breakpoint that covers enough devices so that we don't have to add more than is necessary to our site.

Let's change tack now, but stay with the Apple theme. No, I'm not thinking of food! How many of you are lucky enough to own an iPad? If the answer is yes, then this next demo will be of interest. For many standard devices, we are limited in terms of what resolution we can use when displaying images.

Enter a great trick. How about the ability to display higher-resolution images? We don't need to download anything to help with this. Most modern browsers can do this out of the box; all we need is the appropriate media query to tell browsers when to use them.

Detecting high-resolution image support

The advent (and some may say meteoric rise) of mobile devices has introduced an opportunity, supporting higher resolution images.

Most users can't distinguish individual pixels on standard PCs. When viewed at typical distances, some websites would appear too small to use! Instead, the PC will revert to a more realistic resolution, such as 1,440px.

To give a smoother view, some devices pack in extra pixels; this has the effect of making individual pixels harder to view, and images super crisp in appearance. This was started by Apple, who marketed them as Retina displays; others have begun to follow suit and create devices capable of supporting high-res images.

Thankfully, we don't need expensive iPhones or iPads to add support. We can do this with a media query and use Chrome's Device tool to simulate testing it. To see how, let's create a simple demo that switches between two images of a Phalaenopsis or Moth orchid plant. To tell which image is displayed, each will show the resolution in the top right corner of the image:

1. To start, fire up your normal text editor, then add the following code and save it as `min-resolution.css`:

```
<!DOCType html>
<html>
<head>
  <meta charset="utf-8">
  <link rel="stylesheet" type="text/css"
    href="css/min-resolution.css">
</head>
<body>
  <div id="orchid"></div>
</body>
</html>
```

2. Go ahead and create a separate folder called `css`. In it, save the following code as `min-resolution.css`:

```
#orchid {
  background-image: url('../img/mothorchid.png');
  height: 24.31rem;
  width: 36.5rem;
}

@media (min-resolution: 120dpi) {
  #orchid {
    background-image: url('../img/mothorchid@2x.png');
    height: 24.31rem;
    width: 36.5rem;
  }
}
```

3. We also need an images folder. Create this as `img` at the same level as the `css` folder.

4. From the code download that accompanies this book, extract copies of `mothorchid.png` and `mothorchid@2x.png`, then save them into the `img` folder. *Don't change their names!*

5. Go ahead and preview the results of our file. If all is well, we will see something akin to this screenshot:

6. To confirm what size is shown, first activate the Developer toolbar by pressing *Ctrl + Shift + I*. Then enable device mode by pressing *Ctrl + Shift + M*. We will see a toolbar similar to this appear:

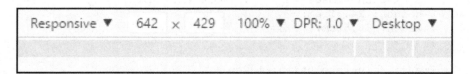

There are two points of note here—one is the setting on the left (**Responsive**), while the other is DPR or device pixel ratio. To trigger displaying the higher resolution image, try changing the setting on the left to **iPhone 6 Plus**:

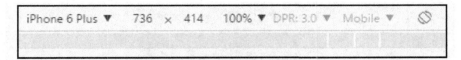

Notice how the DPR setting has jumped to 3.0, and that our image has changed:

Hopefully, you will agree that this is a simple way to add support. Using Chrome, we can get a good representation of how a high-res image will appear; it is worth noting that it should still be tested on a proper device, as even Google can't entirely emulate specific devices from within their browser!

Exploring how it works

At this point, I am sure you will be asking how this all works. It's a simple trick. The key to it is the naming convention we used for the images at the beginning of the demo.

Remember how I said they should be saved as they are from the code download, and to not change the names? The reason for this is that we make use of this in our demo. Apple devices (since iOS4) expect to see the @2x in the filenames to denote a high-res image:

```
1   #orchid {
2     background-image: url('../img/mothorchid.png');
3     height: 24.31rem;
4     width: 36.5rem;
5   }
6
7   @media (min-resolution: 120dpi) {
8     #orchid {
9       background-image: url('../img/mothorchid@2x.png');
10      height: 24.31rem;
11      width: 36.5rem;
12    }
13  }
```

We then make use of that with our media query, which is only set to display the higher resolution image, if our `min-resolution` was detected to be `120dpi` or greater.

 As an aside, you may see `min/max-device-pixel-ratio` being used. This is required to support recent versions of Safari. All other browsers can use min-resolution without issue, although not all support the `dppi` or `dpcm` unit formats that can also be used.

The power of media queries means we can tailor support for higher resolution images to those devices that can support them; if the device is not able to do so, then standard resolution images can be displayed instead.

Okay, let's change tack now. Although writing media queries is a straightforward task, there may be instances where even the best developer doesn't get it quite right! This could be anything from missing the viewport tag to inadvertently writing queries that clash with each other. Let's take a moment to explore some of the more common points where we might trip up, and take a look at a few pointers to help get us back on track.

Examining some common mistakes

When creating sites, and in particular, those that are responsive, it is easy to make mistakes; after all, it's like learning any new technology; we're not perfect from the outset!

To help with your first few steps into the world of responsive construction and creating media queries, let's spend a little time exploring some of the more common mistakes, understand why they cause issues, and go through a few pointers to help avoid these problems:

- **Not including the viewport tag**: This is one of the most common errors to make. When working on mobile devices, we have to include this tag if we want them to be displayed without zooming:

  ```
  <meta name="viewport" content="width=device-width, initial-scale=1">
  ```

  If the tag is not included, then text will appear smaller, as mobile devices zoom pages by default.

- **Syntax errors**: Yes, this old chestnut is another common cause of problems! Hard as it may seem, but mistyping a query can throw up errors, especially for those new to writing media queries. There is no right or wrong answer here. It's a matter of taking care when writing the code; copying and pasting. Take a look at the CSS Media Queries site (at http://cssmediaqueries.com/) for plenty of examples you can use.

- **Inclusive media queries**: Take a look at these two queries for a moment. At first glance, they look perfectly reasonable, don't they? After all, both are set for screen display only and will only show when the screen size is above 767px:

  ```
  @media screen and (max-width: 767px) {
    h1 {
    font-size: 30px;
    }
  }
  @media screen and (min-width: 767px) {
    h1 {
    font-size: 40px
    }
  }
  ```

Trouble is, we still have an issue here. If we set both of these queries in our style sheet, then they will both kick in if our screen estate is 767px or greater. At best, we might end up with h1 being 40px (instead of 30px); at worst, we will get some odd effects! It pays to take care over what media queries you set. Make sure that your queries do not overlap.

- **Specificity and order of inheritance**: Staying with the theme of duplicated selectors (in a sense), another trap that can trip us up is that of inheritance. Say, for example, we specify these two attributes:

```
h3 {color: darkred; }
h3 {color: #f00; }
```

What color will we have? Well, if you said dark red, then get ready for a surprise; the answer is actually #f00 or green. Why would this cause us an issue? If we had written a couple of media queries, but didn't take care over the breakpoints or didn't plan the order of our queries properly, then we might end up adding one too many assignments. Remember, if two selectors apply to the same element, the one with higher specificity wins.

It's all too easy to overthink an issue when working with media queries. In many cases, it simply requires a little forethought and care, and we can produce some useful rules to manage our content on mobile devices without too much overlap.

Let's change tack and move on. Assuming any code we write is syntactically correct, now is a good opportunity to explore some guidelines we can follow when writing media queries. Although the next section is entitled *Exploring best practices*, I personally hate the phrase. It is one which is used and abused to death! Instead, consider them as some friendly tips to help improve your nascent skills when writing queries. It's all about exploring the art of possible, while balancing it with catering for more practical needs, such as our target market and supported devices.

Exploring best practices

Ugh, using this phrase makes me cringe! All too frequently, too many people come up with what they consider to be best practice when talking about subject X or topic Y.

This said, there are some useful tips we can use when creating media queries; they aren't just about following best practice, but equally making things easier for ourselves, so that we can display the right content on the right device at the right time:

- Always start small when designing media queries. This will avoid browsers downloading unnecessary elements that are only needed for larger screen sizes. Starting large is possible, but often requires some heavy reduction of content and is not likely to be as easy to manage.

- When designing queries, don't immediately think you have to include everything from the desktop site on a mobile device. Sometimes it doesn't make sense to do so. More often than not, there simply isn't space or bandwidth to do so! It's important to consider the context of the site you're building for, to ensure you include everything that is suitable or appropriate.

- Give plenty of thought to how content should be prioritized. For example, on a blog site, we frequently see images against article teasers. These won't transfer well to smaller screens, so consider removing these images and leave details of the article, when it was written, author's photo, and the likes. We can still get our message across, but this time just by making some simple tweaks to our design.

- Take care when using media queries with images. Page sizes are on the increase, so it is vitally important that we reference the right image in our queries. Equally, if we have effects such as carousels in place, then we should consider replacing it with a static image; this means we can significantly decrease the size of the page, as a large proportion of the images can be be removed.

- Don't even try to cater for every device available on the market; research in 2015 has shown there to be over 24,000 distinct Android devices, making for a highly fragmented market, which is difficult if not impossible to support in its entirety. Again, server logs will help identify devices being used to access your site. A check through these will identify your top mobile browsers, on which you should focus your efforts.

- When designing, consider using em (or better, rem) units. Pixel values work well for normal design, but do not operate so well when zooming in, which is frequently done with responsive sites. If we use em (or rem) values, this allows the browsers to automatically adjust the design of our site, based on the zoom level in use.

- Make your navigation scalable. Clarity and consistency should rule over similarity to the desktop site. Don't be afraid to use something that is entirely different to the desktop site; clarity and ease of navigation should rule over any other factor, such as color.

- Use icons and fonts where possible, or even SVG images. These scale much better than standard images, particularly if we are using media queries. We can even change the content of the latter using CSS, and still maintain clear images throughout.
- Pay attention to font sizes. We can absolutely use media queries to display larger or smaller fonts, depending on what screen estate is available to us. The key to note though is that if we use percentage values or em/rem units, then these will scale better, and may even remove the need for media queries to handle fonts.
- Watch out for users with visual impairments, such as deuteranopia or color blindness. The available screen viewport on a mobile device will already be smaller; your users will definitely not thank you if font sizes don't scale well, or you've chosen colors that clash, such as white text on a red background!

There is a lot we can accomplish by simply using a text editor, browser, and some careful planning. The great thing though is that we can use media queries to help with many of these tips. It's just a matter of planning so that we don't create more queries than are needed!

Let's move on. Throughout this chapter, we've focused on what is possible when simply using a browser and a text editor to create our queries. I strongly believe that too many simply resort to picking the nearest library to help with constructing our queries; time has come to get back to basics!

This said, there may be instances when we need to use jQuery or a specific library to help produce our queries. A classic example is to incorporate support for older browsers, although it has to be said that it is debatable as to whether we should still support old technology. Assuming though that we have a valid need to use a library, let's spend a moment or two to explore some of the options available to help with creating those queries, that can't be satisfied with simple CSS.

Taking things further

In many instances, we can satisfy our requirements with the use of a text editor and browser; the latter's device mode (or responsive mode) will play a big part in creating perfectly valid queries that will suit many sites.

However, there will be occasions where this won't be enough. We may need to rely on additional help to support media queries for a particular project. One must ask, though, if this is really necessary, and not simply an excuse to be lazy. The media query support in recent browsers is very solid!

This said, if we have to use outside help, then there are plenty of options available online. Let's take a look at a few examples:

- **Plain JavaScript or jQuery**: It goes without saying, but most solutions will be based on either of these two technologies; these will, of course, be obvious choices! The point to note, though, is that jQuery was always designed to complement sites, and not play a core part in their design; one might argue that creating media queries is not a good use of jQuery for this reason.

- **.resizr** (`http://resizr.co/`): This website is one of many we can use to get a feel for how well our site might work on a range of mobile devices; it does rely on you having a site that is accessible to the Internet, and there is no substitute for the real thing! It is a good start though, so when you get to test your site on real devices, it should mean that many of the basic issues have been resolved.

- **What's My Device Pixel Ratio?**: Hosted at `http://devicepixelratio.com/`, this tool works out what your screen's device ratio setting is capable of supporting. This is perfect for those instances where we may want to use high-res images. After all, there is no point using them if your chosen device can't display them!

- **Mediaqueri.es**: Hosted at `http://mediaqueri.es/`, this website should be in any developer's armory. It is a display of inspirational sites that use media queries and RWD.

- **Modernizr**: Available from `http://www.modernizr.com`, we can use the library to test for media query support; an alternative is to use the `@supports` directive. In most cases, it will be older versions of IE that cause issues. If we plan our site with care, we may be able to design out the need for either, by providing a base site that works in IE, and adding extra touches on top for other browsers.

- **Restive.js**: From `http://restivejs.com/`, this jQuery-based plugin is a real Swiss Army knife of functionality, and allows you to add responsive support for different aspects of your sites.

- **Responsive design patterns**: The agency Code My Views, based in the USA, created a number of patterns for use in responsive design; this may be worth a look once you are more accustomed to working with media queries. You can see more details at `https://codemyviews.com/blog/5-really-useful-responsive-web-design-patterns`.

Whichever way you decide to go, there are plenty of options available online, to help with developing your media queries. The key here though is to be sure that if you are adding an additional library, then it is the right thing to do for your site; it will probably center around whether your project must support old browsers such as IE8. This browser has been around since 2009, and should really be put out to pasture—permanently!

Summary

Creating media queries opens up a world of possibilities; we are not forced to have to display every element of our page on each device, so we can be selective about what we show our visitors, depending on which device they use! We've covered a number of useful techniques in this chapter by just using a browser and text editor, so let's take a moment to recap what we've learned.

We kicked off with a quick interactive demo, to illustrate how some well-known sites have used media queries to realign content on screen, before exploring how media queries are constructed.

We then took a look at some of the different types. This included covering both the media types and features we can use to control how content is displayed. We then moved onto looking at some common breakpoint statements that we might use in our code, before exploring how we might need to create custom breakpoints for specific purposes. We also saw how we may even be able to reduce or remove breakpoints, if we make some simple changes to our code.

Next up came a more practical look at using media queries. We explored how we can use them to make content on a simple page display properly in a mobile device (allowing its orientation). We then covered how we can use media queries to control whether we display images of standard or higher resolution on screen.

We then rounded off the chapter with a look at fixing some common mistakes that we might make, before covering some of the options available that we can step up to using once we're more accustomed to creating media queries for our sites.

Phew, we've come to the end of the technical development; there is one more topic we should cover as part of our journey through creating responsive sites. There is no point in creating solutions if they are not efficient. Your visitors will not thank you if it takes an age to load a site! We can fix this with some simple tips and tricks, as part of optimizing our code. We'll explore this topic, and more, in the next chapter.

5

Testing and Optimizing for Performance

Throughout the course of this book, we've explored some of the essentials of responsive web design, using HTML5 and CSS3, and learned how to begin to modify our code to make content responsive across different devices.

We should keep in mind that building just a responsive website is not enough—we must also test and optimize content to work as efficiently as possible across different devices. If pages on our site are slow to load, then this will clearly be a concern. Throughout the course of this chapter, we will look at some of the tips and tricks we can use to begin to ensure that our sites are sufficiently responsive and content loads quickly.

In this chapter, we will cover the following topics:

- Exploring why pages load slowly
- Optimizing the performance of our sites
- Measuring site performance
- Testing for cross-browser compatibility
- Exploring best practices

Curious? Let's get started!

Understanding the importance of speed

The advent of using different devices that can access the Internet means speed is critical—the time it takes to download content from hosting servers and how quickly the user can interact with the site are key to the success of any site.

Why it is important to focus on the performance of our website on the mobile devices or those devices with lesser screen resolution? There are several reasons for this, they include the following:

- Nearly 80 percent of Internet users own a smartphone
- Around 90 percent of users go online through a mobile device, with 48% of users using search engines to research new products
- Approximately 72 percent of users abandon a website if the loading time is more than 5–6 seconds
- Mobile digital media time is now significantly higher compared to desktop use

If we do not consider statistics such as these, then we may go ahead and construct our site, but end up with a customer losing both income and market share, if we have not fully considered the extent of where our site should work. Coupled with this is the question of performance; if our site is slow, then this will put customers off and contribute to lost sales.

A study performed by San Francisco-based Kissmetrics shows that mobile users wait between 6–10 seconds before they close the website and lose faith in it. At the same time, tests performed by Guy Podjarny for the Mediaqueri.es website (`http://mediaqueri.es`) indicate that we're frequently downloading the same content for both large and small screens; this is entirely unnecessary when, with some simple changes, we can vary content to better suit desktop PCs or mobile devices!

So, what can we do? Well, before we start exploring where to make changes, let's take a look at some of the reasons why sites run slowly.

Understanding why pages load slowly

Although we may build a great site that works well across multiple devices, it's still no good if it is slow! Every website will of course operate differently, but there are a number of factors to allow for, which can affect page (and site) speed:

- **Downloading data unnecessarily**: On a responsive site, we may hide elements that are not displayed on smaller devices; the use of `display: none` in code means that we still download content, even though we're not showing it on screen, resulting in slower sites and higher bandwidth usage.

- **Downloading images before shrinking them**: If we have not optimized our site with properly sized images, then we may end up downloading images that are larger than necessary on a mobile device. We can of course make them fluid by using percentage-based size values, but if the original image is still too large, this places extra demand on the server and browser to resize them.
- **A complicated DOM in use on the site**: When creating a responsive site, we have to add in a layer of extra code to manage different devices; this makes the DOM more complicated and slows our site down. It is, therefore, imperative that we don't add any any unnecessary elements that require additional parsing time by the browser.
- **Downloading media or feeds from external sources**: It goes without saying that these are not under our control; if our site is dependent on them, then the speed of our site will be affected if these external sources fail.
- **Use of Flash**: Sites that rely heavy on using Flash will clearly be slower to access than those that don't use the technology. It is worth considering if our site really needs to use it; recent changes by Adobe mean that Flash as a technology is being retired in favor of animation using other means such as HTML5 Canvas or WebGL.

There is one other point to consider, which we've not covered in this list; the average size of a page has significantly increased since the dawn of the Internet in the mid-nineties. Although these figures may not be 100% accurate, they still give a stark impression of how things have changed:

- **1995**: At that time, the average page size used to be around 14.1 KB. The reason for it can be that it contained around two or three embedded objects such as images. That meant just two or three calls to the server on which the website was hosted.
- **2008**: The average page size increased to around 498 KB in size, with an average use of around 70 objects that includes changes to CSS, images, and JavaScript. Although this is tempered with the increased availability of broadband, not everyone can afford fast access, so we will lose customers if our site is slow to load.

All is not lost though—there are some tricks we can use to help optimize the performance of our sites. Many of these apply equally to standard sites as well as responsive ones—let's take a look in more detail.

Optimizing the performance

So far, we've explored some of the reasons why our site might be slow, and the consequences we face if we do not address performance issues. Although some of the issues we could face may not be easy to solve, we can still effect changes that help improve performance of our sites.

Starting with Google

Analysis shows that if a page takes longer than 4–5 seconds to load, then customers will frequently vote with their feet (that is, walk away). Any delay of more than a second can equally lead to a poor user experience.

A great source that can help us understand where some of our issues are is that behemoth, Google. We may knock it for being omnipotent, but it clearly knows some useful tricks!

Google states that our page doesn't have to entirely load within 4–5 seconds, but should be usable within this time; any content that is of a lower priority can be put below the fold or loaded in the background.

At a basic level, Google recommends that our server response time should be less than 200 ms—we should also explore aspects such as client-side rendering to help reduce the time taken to load our content:

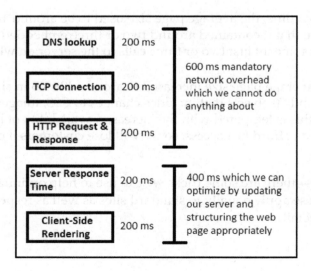

Although much of this applies to any site, this is particularly important for responsive sites, given the extra code required to manage the experience for mobile devices.

Google also recommends that we should consider performing these tasks:

- Minimize the number of redirections and roundtrips required to render content
- Optimize JavaScript execution and image sizes
- Avoid external blocking of the JavaScript and CSS in above-the-fold content, by pushing scripts to the bottom of the page
- Reduce the number of domains called from a page, which helps avoid redirection between mobile and desktop clients

In addition, we can explore the use of other tricks to help with performance. These include the following:

- **Use of cache**: We can consider using this as a means to store data temporarily, that doesn't change very often; it will help reduce the number of requests to the server (and consequently bandwidth usage), if the content hasn't changed. With the advent of HTML5, we can even use the offline AppCache facility. This has the added bonus of making content available offline, if our Internet access fails. A similar technique exists with local storage; while this is not available offline by default, it can be used to cache more persistent content if needed.
- **Use of Scalable Vector Graphics (SVGs)**: Unlike JPEG or PNG images, these can resize without loss of quality, so are perfect for responsive designs; their size is often smaller than an equivalent standard image. These will not suit every application though, as their use is more suited for line drawings or logos.
- **Apply fragment caching**: If we're generating dynamic pages that require server resources to render but where only a small part changes, then applying fragment caching means we can store static versions of the content that doesn't change. When a page is then requested, we send the cached content, and only apply the changes needed to update the content. This reduces the number of calls to our database backend and therefore the resources required to display our content.
- **Optimize the database**: If our website is one where content is posted from different sources, then content will be updated frequently; garbage data will equally increase. We should spend time regularly cleaning content in our database to ensure it is as small and working as efficiently as possible.

Taking things further

If we want to explore things further, then there are some more advanced, invasive changes we can use to help optimize our site. These involve more work, so should be planned as longer term changes:

- **Enabling GZip compression**: We can use this to compress resources, which will make pages load faster. However, this shouldn't be applied across a site without planning; some elements such as CSS or JavaScript can be compressed or minified during development, so applying GZip compression will not result in any benefits.

- **Choosing our host**: There are dozens of hosts available; each will offer different levels of functionality and performance that can have an impact on the operation of our site. It's important to take time to choose the right host; it's worth comparing different hosts to see how they fare, and get recommendations from others as to who has performed well over longer periods of time.

> Check `http://www.whoishostingthis.com` for reviews on companies and see how they stack up against others.

- **Excluding content or media that is not required**: This should almost be self-explanatory, but we should not load content that isn't needed! It's key to understand client requirements; if clients insist on making everything available from both desktop and mobile devices, then it may be necessary to take them through the reasons why this isn't a good course of action and encourage them to see that providing less content on a mobile device won't necessarily result in a poor user experience.

- **Exploring the use of Content Delivery Networks (CDNs)**: This helps render content more quickly, as it is fetched from the nearest local server to the client. Content is normally uploaded to one central point, but is then replicated to several key servers around the world; this reduces the distance travelled and time taken to render content on the screen.

- **Limiting HTTP requests**: As a part of development, we should consider the number of HTTP requests that our site will have to make to the server and aim to reduce these as much as possible. This reduction will help toward reducing network traffic and improving performance, as we do not have to access the DOM as frequently, nor wait as long for content to be downloaded. We can use tools such as creating image sprites or pre-processors to merge multiple CSS files into one, to help with keeping HTTP requests to a minimum.

It takes time to optimize a site, but the effort spent in refining it will pay dividends in increased patronage and ultimately increased sales. The trouble is, we won't know how well our site performs unless we test it; let's explore some of the tools we can use to help gauge how well our site is operating, in more detail.

Testing the performance of our site

We built our responsive pages, improved the look and feel, and also optimized the performance of our site. But before the application goes live, it is the duty of a developer (or dedicated tester) to test the performance of the website.

There is a set of tools that we can use:

- **mobiReady** (http://ready.mobi/): This free tool is used for testing the performance of a responsive website across different resolutions in parallel. It gives each page a score out of five, based on factors such as data sent or received and number of requests made.
- **Webpagetest** (http://www.webpagetest.org/): This online tool helps in testing the performance of a website with respect to specific location and browser for which we want the result. We can test a page for a number of different factors, such as caching static content, effective use of CDN, or if keep alive has been enabled.
- **Google's Pagespeed Insights Tool** (https://developers.google.com/speed/pagespeed/insights/): With this tool we can do the speed analysis of our responsive website for both desktop and mobile versions of the site. This tool rates the website out of 100 for the speed and user experience, providing a list of pointers we can fix, along with details on how they can be fixed.
- **IntoDns.com** (http://www.intodns.com/): Although this is not a performance testing tool as such, it can help determine if the performance of our site is affected, as a result of issues with our DNS. It provides a report of the website and mail servers, which we can use to fix issues and ultimately help keep performance at peak efficiency.
- **YSlow** (http://yslow.org/): This bookmarklet grades any chosen website into either one of three predefined rulesets or a custom one we define. It offers suggestions for where we can improve the page's performance, based on an array of different values, such as DNS lookups, making AJAX cacheable, avoiding CSS expressions, and configuring eTags.

These are some useful tools, which can help with performance and optimization of our site (with plenty more available online). However, we are missing out on an opportunity, if we focus purely on these tools. What about using what is already available in our browser?

Most (if not all) browsers have some form of DOM inspector built in to the browser or available as a standalone option. These can provide some good information that we can use as a precursor to more in-depth details from external services. To see what is possible, let's explore what we can get if we run a simple check on a website in a DOM inspector; for this example, we will use that doyenne of online retail, Amazon; it has sites available all over the world. We will perform the same test twice: the first one will be as a desktop browser and the second as an (emulated) mobile version, using Chrome's built-in DOM inspector.

Working through a desktop example

For our test, we'll start with a desktop browser—we'll use Google's Chrome as it has a good set of tools; other browsers can also be used, but you may not get quite the same results. Let's make a start, using Amazon as the basis for our test:

Here's what we need to do:

1. Fire up Chrome, then press *Shift + Ctrl + I* to display the Developer toolbar.
2. Look for the red record button toward the top left of the window, then click on it.
3. Revert back to Chrome's window, then browse to `http://www.amazon.com`. As soon as the page has finished loading, click on the red record button to stop recording.

At this point, we will have a set of results we can browse through, similar to this extract:

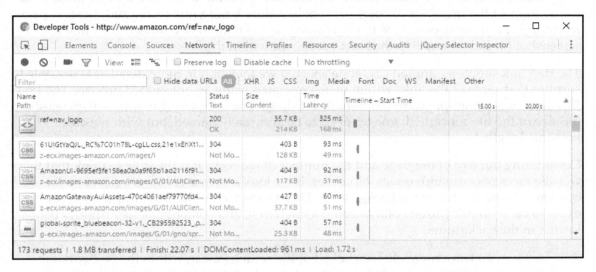

At first, these results may not make sense, but the details we want are at the foot of the window.

173 requests | 1.8 MB transferred | Finish: 22.07 s | DOMContentLoaded: 961 ms | Load: 1.72 s

This shows the number of server requests made, the amount of content transferred, and the times taken to initially parse the DOM (DOMContentLoaded); then, fully download the content (indicated by **Finish** and the **Load** event being fired).

 Note that the DOMContentLoaded time relates to parsing the document only, and does not allow for whether other resources such as scripts, images, or external style sheets have been downloaded.

Even though Amazon's site downloads a reasonable amount of content, they've made good use of some of the tricks we've covered, to help reduce bandwidth usage and increase page rendering speed. How can we tell? Try clicking on the bottom two links shown in the screenshot (or links 4 and 5 in the asset list shown within the browser).

The first link shows a minified CSS style sheet; if we look at it in more detail, it is possible to surmise that some of the links within were generated using an automated process. The PNG filename in one example is over 70+ characters long! The use of long names will increase the file size of the file concerned; images need to be accurately named, but with sensible filename lengths!

Considering the size of the page and the number of requests, it is possible to think that this website faces performance issues. However, if we look more carefully, we can see a lot of content is being loaded in the background. This means we're still providing a good user experience, with prioritized content being loaded first, and content of lesser priority being loaded in the background.

 To learn more about what all of the settings mean within the Network tab of Chrome's developer toolbar, take a look at the main documentation on the Google Developer's site, at http://bit.ly/2ay9H8g.

Let's change track now, and focus on viewing the same site on a mobile device—this time the iPhone 6 Plus.

Viewing on a mobile device

We perform the same test again, but this time set Chrome to emulate an iPhone 6 Plus, then we should see this:

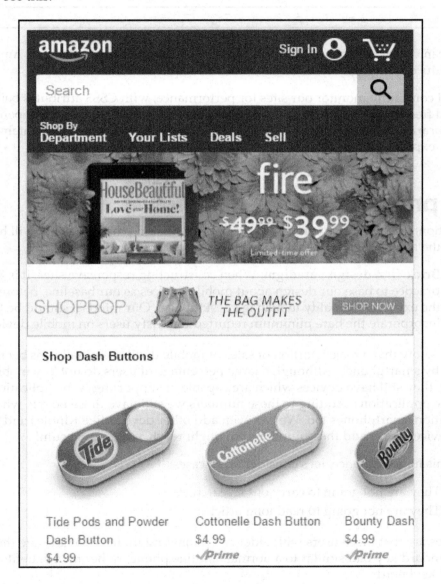

The real test though is in the number of requests made, amount of data transferred, and the time taken to load the page. This time around, our browser made 103 requests, with 1.8 MB transferred from the server and completed the total download in approximately 12 seconds:

103 requests | 1.8 MB transferred | Finish: 11.74 s | DOMContentLoaded: 1.37 s | Load: 2.09 s

Here, we can clearly see that to provide best user experience to its customers, Amazon has cleverly reduced the page size and the number of requests.

We should constantly monitor our sites for performance; with CSS3 attributes being added or updated frequently, we can begin to update our site and start to remove dependencies on external libraries, which allows us to increase the speed of our site and ultimately provide a better user experience.

Best practices

In this section, you will learn some of the best practices and paradigms that will help us in achieving the actual goals of web development:

- **Brick-first design paradigm**: When constructing responsive sites, it is better practice to base our design about mobile devices as our baseline, before adding the extra functionality to manage desktop use. Our mindset should be to incorporate the bare minimum required to satisfy users on mobile devices.

Today, we know that a major portion of sales of mobile devices annually has been overtaken by smartphones. Although a large percentage of users do not buy mobile devices frequently, they still have devices which are capable of supporting web applications and even native applications. Adding to these numbers we still have those people who use some old generation smartphones too. We can even add other devices like Kindles and semi web-capable devices; if we add these numbers we might reach a staggering sum!

Now for this huge audience, let's consider some cases:

- They are not going to carry out research
- They are not going to read long articles

The chances are that those users with older cell phones might have to navigate the page using a standard key pad similar to a normal landline phone, rather than benefit from using a standard keyboard.

The small size of screens on older devices makes it harder to provide a mobile-first layout; it makes it ever more important that we only display the bare essentials for these users, and that other elements are removed from display or download.

Providing support for older browsers

Another best practice to follow to improve the performance of our website for those old devices, which have limited functionalities and are not as fast as today's mobile devices.

We know that since we have the Internet, we have web browsers to display the content. We should not forget that there are users who still use older mobile devices and which lack the features of modern equivalents; we can handle this using graceful degradation.

Graceful degradation is a strategy, which is used to handle the design of web pages for different browsers. If we built a website using the graceful degradation strategy, then it is intended to be viewed first by the modern browsers and then in the old browsers, which have less features. It should degrade in such a way that our website still looks good with respect to look and feel and is still functional but with less features.

 Note that graceful degradation does not mean that we are telling our users to download the most recent browser to view our website.

But today's modern designers and developers do not like this approach. The main reason is that it often turns into a demand where our users should download the most recent and updated browser in order to view the best view of our website. We should remember that this is not graceful degradation.

If we are asking our users to download a modern browser, then that means we are using a browser-centric approach. Some points we should remember to follow for graceful degradation, which can equally apply to progressive enhancement:

- We should write HTML, which is valid and standard compliant
- We should use external style sheets
- We should always link our scripts externally
- We should always make sure that our content is accessible for old browsers without CSS or JavaScript

Considering which features to support

When developing responsive sites, we should check to see if our target browser or device can support a specific feature, rather than simply assuming it can be used.

For example, if we were to install the latest Chrome browser on an old Android phone, we might be tempted to assume that it will support the latest features, such as CSS animations, background parallax effects, and WebGL.

But, is this really the case? What would happen if we were to try to operate a site that relied on a feature that is not supported on an older Android device? The end result might be that our browser becomes unresponsive or crash; we would be forced to have to reboot it to restore service.

This issue was faced by Android users recently in a big way and in this the most noticeable application to suffer was Google Talk/Hangout. With their upgrade, the most lightweight chat service of Google was turned to an almost unusable application due to performance issues on the older devices.

This way it is really important to filter out those features, which are less usable and have less relevance on small screens. A great example is the applications that make use of proximity sensors. This helped push manufacturers to make this a standard feature across all newer smartphones.

Let the user choose what they want

We developed an eye-catching, responsive, animated, and touch-oriented website but for a user who has poor Internet connection or an old device?

What should we do if the site appears to be hanging during the initial load or on subsequent page refreshes?

The reader will of course be confused as to what they should do.

Here is a simple thing we should do. Ever run Gmail on an old device or slow Internet connection? If yes, then you must have noticed **Load basic HTML (for slow connections)**, or even this gem, where slower connections mean we may be forced to use Gmail's simple view, because a slow Internet connection makes using the standard view impossible:

For the elite few who are used to high-speed cable or broadband connections, they may find it hard to believe that other users do not have that luxury, and are forced to use the basic view, as would be the case in our example. Using this option loads the basic GUI version of Gmail, which is optimized for slower connections, and allows the user to interact with the site.

This illustrates a great point—if a site must use the latest features, then we should consider implementing a basic or standard mode in our application. We progressed from the days of a select few sites that have all of the latest features and which get all of the traffic, providing a user with what they are looking for on the website is what they care about.

Do we need to include a whole library?

We should always follow the standard of either *use it* or *keep it*. It is difficult to keep track of all the libraries and modules which are in use; we have to strike a fine balance between the libraries we use and maintaining site speed.

Many frameworks and libraries now have the option to customize the functionality provided within; for example, we may only require key elements of jQuery (if we were using it); we can select to exclude redundant functionality when downloading the library. However, if we are still at a development phase, then we will require the whole library; we can choose the parts needed to run our application, before minifying it for production use.

Considering cross-browser compatibility

A question that must always be at the back of the minds of any developer is how to retain maximum browser compatibility when constructing sites; it does not matter if the UI is stunning, if it doesn't work on enough browsers!

Any site that does not support its target browser market (that is, those browsers most used by the site's audience), risks losing business and reputation. This makes it even more important that we not only test our site, but test it across multiple browsers if we're making it responsive. This testing is a key step to retaining customer satisfaction and market share. There are a number of techniques we can use to help reduce issues related to cross-browser compatibility, before we consider some of the solutions available, let's look at some of the challenges we face in more detail.

Outlining the challenges

The utopia for any designer is to have a 100% bug-free site; the reality though is that while this will always be at the back of the developer's mind, it is impossible to achieve!

Why? One key consideration is the use of CSS3 (and those elements of CSS4 that now exist); although support is constantly improving, there is still a way to go before every browser offers consistent support for all CSS3 attributes. In the same vein, support for responsive media and media queries are not supported by older browsers, so we must consider how much support we can afford to offer for these browsers.

Considering possible solutions, we've touched on three elements which are key considerations for responsive sites, to work around them, there are a number of options open to us.

We can (and should) consider constructing our site using the base content that will work on any browser; we can then progressively enhance the experience, by adding extra features that may only work for some browsers, but are not key to the overall user experience. In comparison, we could take the view that we build our site around the latest technologies and browsers, but then add in support to allow content to degrade gracefully, when used on older browsers.

Can we work around these issues? Absolutely, there are a number of different options on offer. There is one point we should consider though, using a JavaScript solution isn't necessarily the best solution; there are a number of tips and tricks we can use to help retain compatibility. Before we touch on these, let's take a moment to consider some of the options available when using JavaScript as a solution:

- **Adapt.js**: This script doesn't use media queries; instead, it works out which CSS file to load, based on values such as the browser's window size. This script can be downloaded from `http://adapt.96.gs/`.

- **Modernizr.js**: This library allows us to pick and choose elements we want to support, such as HTML5 `<video>` elements; when chosen elements are detected as being in use, Modernizr provides us with an option to gracefully degrade content, and not let our site simply fall into a heap! The library is available from `https://modernizr.com/download`.

- **Respond.js**: This solution uses JavaScript to provide breakpoint support for older browsers (such as IE6-8), based on the sizes we specify when configuring our pages. We can use it in a similar way to standard CSS-based breakpoints, such as setting device-width to 414px, to cater for an iPhone 6 Plus in portrait mode. More details and downloads of the library are available from `http://responsejs.com/`.

Although these solutions will work perfectly well, they all suffer from one inherent drawback—JavaScript! In this modern age, most browsers are likely to have this switched on by default, but there will be instances where this is not the case; let's explore why using JavaScript isn't always the right solution.

Understanding the drawbacks of JavaScript

During the construction phase of any responsive site, we will naturally need to work out which breakpoints we want to support. This will be based on statistics such as Google Analytics. The normal route would then be to use media queries in our CSS style sheet to load elements when needed. This works fine for recent browsers (anything within the last year to eighteen months), but with older browsers this will prove an issue.

We can support them using JavaScript-based solutions:

- All of the solutions we've touched on need JavaScript– if it's switched off, then they clearly won't work!
- Some of the solutions use AJAX to fetch content (such as Adapt.js). This can show a brief flash when getting the content. The developers have tried to reduce this to the absolute minimum, but no matter how much they try, it will be impossible to get rid of it; it will look odd when used on a site.
- Some of the solutions won't work on older devices, Adapt.js being a good example.
- We can use a default style sheet if JavaScript is switched off, using `<no script>` tags; the question is, what screen size do we support?
- Using JavaScript will require the server to load additional resources, which places additional demand on the server; JavaScript was always designed to provide additional functionality, and shouldn't be used when that functionality is key to the successful operation of a site.

Clearly these drawbacks make for a less attractive option when using JavaScript! Two key questions we should ask though are: do we really need to support older browsers, such as IE8, and use JavaScript to support them?

Providing a CSS-based solution

The question of which browsers to support is one that will divide both developers and designers; on one hand, we will have creatives that want to take advantage of the latest functionality, while others will state that we must support as wide a browser population as possible.

The latter might normally require the use of JavaScript for older browsers; given that this requires extra resources that we must call from the server, it makes sense to use CSS where possible. To this end, we can consider using the relatively new `@supports` feature, (or feature queries, to give it its technical name). This works in a similar way to media queries and allows us to style elements based on whether the chosen style is supported in the browser. This has gained great support in most recent browsers (except of course IE, which always likes to be different!):

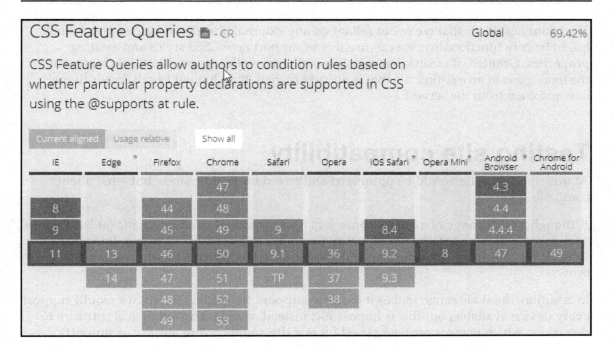

We can then create code such as this in the main markup:

```
<article class="artwork">
  <img src="myimg.jpg" alt="cityscape">
</article>
```

And style it using code such as this, when it is supported:

```
@supports (mix-blend-mode: overlay) {
  .artwork img {
    mix-blend-mode: overlay;
  }
}
```

However if it isn't supported, then we simply add a feature query to allow it to gracefully degrade:

```
@supports not(mix-blend-mode: overlay) {
  .artwork img {
    opacity: 0.5;
  }
}
```

The beauty of this is that we're not reliant on any external libraries to help support what might be core functionality; we can use this to support new CSS3 styles and existing properties. Granted, it means that our style code base will increase, but this is tempered as the increase is in an existing file that is already cached, than having to call an additional new resource from the server!

Testing site compatibility

At this stage, our site would be optimized and tested for performance, but what about compatibility?

Although a wide range of available browsers have remained relatively static (at least for the ones in mainstream use), the functionality they offer is constantly changing; this makes it difficult for developers and designers to handle all of the nuances required to support each browser.

In addition, the wide range makes it costly to support. In an ideal world, we would support every device available, but this is impossible; instead, we must use analytical software to determine which devices are being used for our site and therefore worthy of support.

Working out a solution

If we test our site on a device such as an iPhone 6, there is a good chance it will work as well on other Apple devices, such as iPads. The same can be said for testing on a mobile device such as a Samsung Galaxy S4; we can use this principle to help prioritize support for particular mobile devices, if they require more tweaks to be made than in comparison to other devices.

Ultimately though, we must use analytical software to determine who visits our site; the information such as browser, source, OS, and device used will help determine what our target audience should be. This does not mean we completely neglect other devices; we should try to ensure they work with our site too, but this will not be a priority during development.

A key point to note is that we should not attempt to support every device; this is too costly to manage, and we would never keep up with all of the devices available for sale! Instead, we can use our analytics software to determine which devices are being used by our visitors; we can then test a number of different properties:

- **Screen size**: This should encompass a variety of different resolutions for desktop and mobile devices.
- **Connection speed**: Testing across different connection speeds will help us understand how the site behaves and identify opportunities or weaknesses where we may need to effect changes.
- **Pixel density**: Some devices will support higher pixel density, which allows them to display higher resolution images or content. When designing sites (and particularly responsive ones), we clearly want to position our content in the right place on screen. The clarity afforded by high-resolution displays makes it easier to fine-tune how this content is displayed on screen; this will make it easier to view and fix any issues with displaying web content.
- **Interaction style**: The ability to view the Internet across different devices means that we should consider how our visitors interact with the site: is it purely on a desktop, or do they use tablets, smartphones, or gaming-based devices? It's most likely that the former two will be used to an extent, but the latter is not likely to feature as highly.

Once we've determined which devices we should be supporting, then there are a range of tools available for us to use, to test browser compatibility. These include physical devices (ideal, but expensive to maintain), emulators, or online services (these can be commercial or free). Let's take a look at a selection of what is available, to help us with testing browser compatibility.

Exploring tools available for testing

When we plan to test a mobile or responsive website, there are factors which we need to consider before we start testing, to help deliver a website which looks consistent across all the devices and browsers. These factors include answering these three questions:

- Does the website look good?
- Are there any known bugs or defects?
- Is our website really responsive?

To help test our sites, we can use any one of several tools available (either paid or free); a key point to note though, is that we can already get a good idea of how well our sites work, by simply using the Developer toolbar that is available in most browsers!

Granted, it's not something we should absolutely rely on, but it provides a perfect starting point. We can always move up to a commercial option when we've outgrown the capabilities offered in a browser. Let's take a brief look at what's available:

Viewing with Chrome

We can easily emulate a mobile device within Chrome, by pressing *Ctrl + Shift + M*; Chrome displays a toolbar at the top of the window, which allows us to select different devices:

If we click on the menu entry (currently showing iPhone 6 Plus) and change it to Edit, we can add new devices; this allows us to set specific dimensions, user agent strings, and whether the device supports high-resolution images:

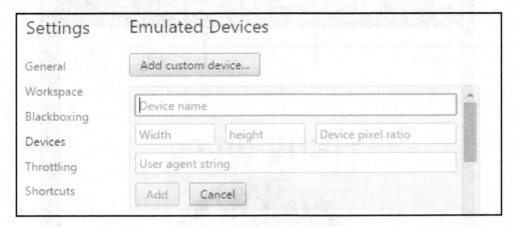

Let's switch now, and take a look at the options available in Firefox.

Working in Firefox

The responsive design view option is available using the same *Ctrl + Shift + M* option as Chrome; we can also access it by navigating to **Tools** | **Web Developer** | **Responsive Design Mode** from the menu.

When the mode is activated in Firefox, we can switch between different screen sizes:

Although browsers can go some way in providing an indication of how well our site works, they can only cater to a limited range of views. Sometimes, we need to take things a step further and use commercial solutions to test our sites across multiple browsers at the same time. Let's take a look at some of the options available commercially.

Exploring our options

If you've spent any time developing code, then there is a good chance you may already be aware of Browserstack (from `https://www.browserstack.com`). Other options include the following:

- **GhostLab**: `https://www.vanamco.com/ghostlab/`
- **Muir**: `http://labs.iqfoundry.com/`
- **CrossBrowserTesting**: `http://www.crossbrowsertesting.com/`

If, however, all we need to do is check our site for its level of responsiveness, then we don't need to use paid options. There are a number of sites that allow us to check, without needing to install plugins or additional tools:

- **Am I Responsive**: `http://ami.responsive.is`
- **ScreenQueries**: `http://screenqueri.es`
- **Cybercrab's screen check facility**: `http://cybercrab.com/screencheck`
- **Remy Sharp's check site**: `http://responsivepx.com`

We can also use bookmarklets to check to see how well our sites work on different devices—a couple of examples to try are at `http://codebomber.com/jquery/resizer` and `http://responsive.victorcoulon.fr/`; it is worth noting that the current browsers already include this functionality, making the bookmarklets less attractive as an option.

Following best practices

A key question we must ask ourselves is to what extent we will support the use of particular browsers when developing our websites. The answer to this will lie in monitoring analytical software, to determine which browsers are being used.

In most cases, it should show modern browsers being used, but there are still limited instances of old browsers in use; for example, IE6 is still being used, although its market share is now a tiny 0.25%, as at April 2016. This raises the question of what we should support, if monitoring analytics for our sites shows that only a tiny percentage (that is, lower than 1%, for example) of usage is for older browsers, then we may take the decision to not support them if the effort and resources required do not justify the return from such a small market share.

This said, there are some basic tips that can help us optimize our sites:

- We should avoid using hacks where possible. Conditional comments are a better option, although we should regularly check and remove styles if they are no longer applicable (such as vendor prefixes, which no longer apply).
- Try to use `<!DOCType html>` in your code. This will indicate to the browser that it should follow HTML5 rules; it will degrade automatically if the browser does not support HTML5.
- We can use the W3C Validation Service to check our code for consistency. A better option though is to build this into part of the development process; we can easily do this with Node.js, so it can be done automatically.
- In the age of modern sites, JavaScript has become an essential tool for development. It is all too easy to resort to using it, without really considering the options available. Try to avoid using JavaScript if possible. It was designed to complement existing code, and should not be relied on to provide core functionality. The state of CSS is such now that styling functionality that previously was only possible with JavaScript may now be feasible with CSS and provide smoother results to boot!

Summary

In this chapter, we learned what performance is and what the consequences are if a website has poor performance. Then, we explored what factors could cause our web page to load slowly. In this chapter, we also learned how we can measure the performance of a website with the help of various tools available online, and covered the steps we can take to improve the performance of our websites. We then covered some of the best practices we can follow with relevance to the performance of the website.

We then moved on to explore the importance of maintaining cross-browser compatibility and considered some of the solutions that are available to deal with cross-browser issues. Then, we covered the challenges that are present in testing cross-browser compatibility across a wide combination of available browsers and devices. Apart from that, we discovered how to tackle this problem and devise a strategy to get the maximum output. Finally, we saw some of the tools that are available online to test the compatibility of our website across various browser-device combinations. We have now reached the end of our journey through the essentials of creating responsive sites. We hope you enjoyed reading this book as much as we have writing it, and that it helps you make a start into the world of responsive design using little more than plain HTML and CSS.

Index

CPSIA information can be obtained
at www.ICGtesting.com
Printed in the USA
LVOW04s0415040817

543477LV00008B/67/P